2400

Unnecessary Suffering

D1210164

Unnecessary Suffering

Managing Market Utopia

MAURICE GLASMAN

VERSO

London • New York

First published by Verso 1996
© Maurice Glasman
All rights reserved

The rights of Maurice Glasman to be identified as the author of
this work have been asserted by him in accordance with the
Copyright, Designs and Patents Act 1988

Verso
UK: 6 Meard Street, London W1V 3HR
USA: 180 Varick Street, New York NY 10014–4606

Verso is the imprint of New Left Books

ISBN 1–85984–976–8
ISBN 1–85984–071–X (pbk)

British Library Cataloguing in Publication Data
A catalogue record for this book is available from the British Library

Library of Congress Cataloging-in-Publication Data
A catalog record for this book is available from the Library of Congress

Typeset by M Rules in Sabon
Printed and bound in Great Britain by
Biddles Ltd, Guildford and King's Lynn

In Memory of Coleman Glasman
Born Limehouse, London, 1927
Died St Bartholomew's Hospital, London, 1995

This One's On Me

Contents

Preface and Acknowledgements

There are two ways in which society acts upon the distinction between necessary and unnecessary suffering. The first is through adopting principles of justice which establish a common status of citizenship for each person, the second concerns the treatment of people at work. While the idea of individual rights has partially succeeded in establishing durable legal institutions, the capacity of society to use moral or democratic categories in its conceptualization of the economy is in disarray. The political philosophy defended in chapter one upholds the priority of individual rights in the constitutional structure of the state and the democratic organization of knowledge and its practical application in the economy. Drawing upon the work of Karl Polanyi, the abstract rules and predictive claims assumed by managerial prerogative are argued to be a threat to the practices of production. A good society, it is claimed, is a society capable of producing goods and a necessary condition of living in such a society is that human beings and nature are not treated as commodities. It is further argued that trust, honesty, courage, solidarity and skill are necessary features of viable economies and the final section of chapter one concentrates on the relationship between the organization of knowledge and technological innovation. Safeguards against exploitation are given the same weight as those that limit oppression.

Chapter two excavates the Catholic and socialist traditions which provided the distinct practices and values that characterized the institutional form of the Federal Republic of Germany after 1945. The tradition of liberal democracy initiated in Paris and Frankfurt in 1848 and carried by the secular and Catholic labour movement throughout the next century combined civil liberties with the democratic organization of work. It was subsequently defeated in each European country in favour of state sovereignty and a competitive economy. With the defeat of Nazism in 1945, however, Christian and Social Democracy provided the cultural orientation characteristic of what became known as the social-market economy. This chapter concentrates on the history of these two movements. It is commonly claimed that the 'Ordo-liberals' of the Freiburg school provided the ideological resources out of which the social-market economy was fashioned and that their ideology was based on fiscal probity and extensive currency reforms. It is argued here that their ideas were far from mainstream economics and their influence has been exaggerated.

Chapter three is an institutional analysis of the social-market economy and the international consensus prevailing after the defeat of Nazism. Significantly different production practices developed in the British and American zones of occupation concerning the status of artisans, trade-union representation on boards of management and the development of works councils within firms; the practices adopted in the British zone were adopted throughout West Germany after 1948. The three distinctive features of the social-market economy, which distinguished the organization of the German economy from other European countries, were co-determination, artisan protection and the democratic administration of pension funds. Co-determination facilitated the most extensively democratic economy in western Europe and shaped the institutions of economic governance until unification in 1990. The protection of the status of artisans in the economy and their function in the training of industrial workers strengthened flexibility and intensified the competitive advantage in national skill formation. The pension scheme is democratically co-determined by labour and capital within each sector of production and offers an alternative to statist welfare strategies.

The central question pursued throughout the book is why the Solidarity movement in Poland, having defeated real existing socialism on the basis of the Catholic and socialist ideas characteristic of the social-market economy, chose market utopianism in its place. The idea that the self-organized institutions of society could democratically resolve the satisfaction of needs and the preservation of culture by subordinating both the state and market to the demands of a decentralized democracy provided the ideological foundation for the practices of labour relations, subsidiarity and federalism characteristic of West Germany after 1948. It was also the ideal around which Polish Solidarity clustered in 1981 through their idea of a self-governing republic.

Solidarity combined the idea of individual rights associated with the social-contract tradition with the democratization of society developed by Catholic and socialist critics of market societies. It is argued in chapter four that while the scale of private property holdings in Poland increased under communist rule, from 74 per cent to 93 per cent of all arable land, the enforcement of managerial prerogative in the economy was consistently upheld. It was in response to managerial authoritarianism that Solidarity deepened and modernized the ideas that underpinned West German reconstruction after Nazism and, as in Germany, the church and the union were the main representatives of societal opposition. The policy adopted after 1989, however, negated the ideas of justice, vocational democracy and the self-governing republic expressed in 1981. The final two chapters of the book are an analysis of why the adoption of a social-market system was not considered a feasible possibility in Poland between 1989 and 1995, when the cultural and institutional preconditions – in the form of the works councils won in the Gdansk Accords of 1981 and a strong trade union and church which shared an ideological orientation with Christian and Social Democracy – were already in place.

Chapter five is a theoretical analysis of the rise of the New Right and the breakdown of the post-war settlement in the United States and Britain in the 1970s. The New Right combined an economic theory which limited welfare, marginalized unions and forbade direct productive interference by the state in the economy with a moral theory that identified the state with oppression and the market with freedom in the sphere of material distribution. Keynesianism and social democracy were attacked on philosophical, political and empirical grounds as undesirable, unpatriotic and unfeasible. The response was confused. While the institutions of regulation and welfare distribution were maintained within western Europe, by the 1980s they were viewed as contingent arrangements and not as necessary elements of social organization in societies characterized by a market economy.

Chapter six uses the conceptual apparatus developed in the previous sections to analyse and describe the reasons why the Solidarity government became the guarantor of the imposition of the most radical blueprint for transition. In their reform programme the neo-classical commissar replaced the old nomenklatura as the prime mover in the economy. Market Leninism is a utopia which shares with its Bolshevik counterpart the elimination of society and its replacement by a managerial vanguard guided by correct theory. The self-governing republic proposed by Solidarity in 1981 was replaced by the notion of corporate governance after 1989. This led to industrial collapse, ethical breakdown and the election of the former Communist Party as the freely chosen representatives of society.

Given the previous absence of a democratically organized society, the international consensus played a critical role in framing the internal possibilities of political action in Poland. The view of the world propounded and enforced by the dominant western states and international institutions imposed conceptual constraints on what could feasibly be achieved by concerted political action. The prevailing definition of the reasonable determined the policy agenda in inappropriate and ultimately unsustainable ways. Western Europe bequeathed the most meagre ideological legacy to those in the East who wished to understand the institutional foundations of the post-war settlement.

The EU, far from admitting its origins in protectionism, racketeering, market rigging and myriad interventions in the form of pig iron quotas and farm subsidies, became indistinguishable from the IMF, World Bank or United States when it came to describing itself and giving advice to other people. This led to a refusal to acknowledge the scale of government intervention, tax levels, educational investment, public transport subsidies, democratic participation and a variety of societal activities undertaken as much as a protection against the effects that market distributions create as a facilitation of their development. All aid to Poland was made conditional on pursuing a reform strategy the likes of which no modern western nation had ever considered imposing on itself for fear of the effects it would have on people's lives and livelihoods.

This book was initially written as a PhD thesis while at the European University Institute in Florence between 1989 and 1995. The people and ideas I came across during the time I lived in Italy formed the immediate context within which this work was composed. Eva Breivik, Marie-Ange Cattotti and Maureen Lechtleitner, the secretaries of the department of social and political science, dealt with all manner of problems and details throughout the five years and my first debt is to them. Without their encouragement and friendship I could never have retained my legal status as a resident, let alone written a book. The library staff, particularly Peter Kennealy, were extremely helpful in ordering books, tracking down articles and procuring obscure data. My supervisor, Steven Lukes, encouraged this book from the outset and provided the material means and intellectual support required for its completion. He was consistently generous and tolerant. Klaus Eder introduced me to aspects of German social theory I would otherwise never have known about. The other three members of my thesis committee, John Gray, Tadeusz Kowalik and Claus Offe, each offered comments which were invaluable in translating the thesis into a book. Throughout this period I was encouraged by the academic service, particularly Andreas Fridjal, which sent me from Moscow to Ljubjana to further my research.

My friends at the EUI made the most important contribution to the finished work. Christoph Dartmann, now at the University of Aberdeen, made his research on German post-war reconstruction available to me at a time when I was only following a hunch. He allowed me access to his laboriously gathered material before it was published. Kees Van Kersbergen, now of the Free University of Amsterdam, read an early article and impressed upon me the importance of Catholic social teaching in both the German post-war settlement and the Solidarity movement in Poland. This opened up a political and philosophical dimension of which I was previously ignorant and the book would have been considerably different without his help. Jeff Weintraub, who was a visiting fellow between 1992 and 1993, read a first draft of the book and insisted that I read Karl Polanyi's *The Great Transformation*. This radically altered the historical framework of analysis, took more than two years to assimilate and delayed publication for even longer. My debt to him is unrepayable. Veronica Muñoz-Dardé, now of University College London, had to endure hours of conversation on the status of work in moral philosophy and indicated ways in which a Kantian conception of rights could be made compatible with the historical analysis I was developing. Philosophy without history is empty, history without philosophy is blind – this seems a trivial conclusion to years of debate but it has been extremely important in the writing of this book. Luisa Zanchi, now of the University of Leeds, brought a micro-economist's rigour to bear on the ideas of supply-side democracy developed in chapters one, three and six and persuaded me that my analysis was compatible with empirical work in contemporary economics and to draw upon it in making my argument. Her contribution was considerable and my appreciation of her and her work is greater than I can say. Perry Anderson, Ian Carter, John Horton, Johan DeDeiken, Glen Newey and Phillipe Van Parijs each helped me in important ways.

My editor at Verso, Robin Blackburn, has been as sympathetic and encouraging as it is possible to be. He sent me relevant books and articles, made extensive comments on the first two drafts and waited patiently for me to finish. Jane Hindle has been welcoming as well as efficient and my copy editor, Jane Raistrick, was equally excellent. I have tried to write in a style that avoids specialized academic jargon and excessive obscurantism. Sometimes the subject matter forbade this and I apologize in advance for the consequent infelicities. The responsibility is mine alone.

Friends outside academia provided material, emotional and intellectual sustenance during the long journey to completion. Mike Lerner was steadfast in his friendship throughout the many episodes which packed these years. Jonathan Karp talked me through many a panic attack. Patrick Hawkins helped me at difficult moments with grace and understanding. Artemis Pittas has been an invaluable ally from the very earliest days. My mother, Rivie Glasman, has been brave and understanding through a grave period of her life.

My overriding debt, however, is to my father, Collie Glasman, who died unexpectedly in January 1995. He came of age with the defeat of Nazism and the election of the Labour government of 1945 and he carried within him many of the virtues of that time. His disdain for consumer gratification and an appreciation of compromise put him at odds with the rigours of the New Right regime and his long wait for a routine operation weakened him so that he did not survive surgery. He served in British Intelligence in Austria between 1945 and 1948 and I first learned of the institutions of the social-market economy from him. Although I initially resisted his appreciation of its efficiency he ultimately won the argument. He was a funny, gentle and brilliant person and with him died an irreplaceable culture and a remarkable man. More than a year later I am still incapable of adjusting to the fact that we will never speak to each other again. I have no religious or spiritual faith, there is life and life only. I dedicate this book to his memory.

1

The Virtue Economy

The Power of Consensus

The distinction between necessary and unnecessary suffering defines the limits of political rationality. In delineating a domain of pain which is amenable to concerted public amelioration from a sphere of grief that is immutable, it defines the power of society to respond to the miseries of life. The enforcement of slavery laws and the denial of medical care to the poor are causes of suffering which have been overcome through political action. The right to an education irrespective of parental preferences for child labour is the result of state interference in what was once considered a familial prerogative, as is the case with the regulation of employment conditions within the private enterprise.

Few claim, for example, that unemployment is good, but if it is understood as necessary in order to keep inflation down, reform incentive structures and encourage foreign investment, then it is an unavoidable fact of life. It cannot be altered by political will. Unemployment may lead to the destruction of inherited skills within society and cause a sense of worthlessness in the unemployed person.[1] If both economic growth and political liberty are threatened by its diminishment, then the individual and society have to find ways of absorbing the dereliction that unemployment brings. It is necessary suffering. What for some is an unbearable dislocation is for others an unavoidable cost of economic

---

1. For detailed data on the miserable state of mind of the unemployed see Andrew Harvey, 'Four Pieces of the Unemployment Puzzle', manuscript presented at the Royal Economics Society, Southampton 1995.

improvement. Whether it is one or the other depends on the political consensus that prevails.

A political consensus is an understanding of the world shared between dominant public agents resulting in durable institutions which structure the distribution of power and goods within society. It is built around those aspects of the world which are held to be unalterable. The significance of a consensus shift in politics, such as the victory of the New Right in the 1980s or the election of Roosevelt in 1932, is that it redefines the scope of public agency through establishing a new framework within which political success and failure can be judged. While an institutionalized consensus justifies the distribution of power, status and knowledge within society there are always dissenters. The secret police and army could not save the Shah from the consequences of twelve years of successful market reforms.[2] The considerable repressive apparatus of Bolshevik regimes collapsed beneath the weight of their rising literacy and infant survival rates.[3] Politics is here understood primarily as a public struggle over the definition of sanity. It is through the successful definition of alternatives as insane that the power of a consensus is maintained. In the setting of agendas the reasonable organizes the rational.[4] Prices are not the only factor depending on people's assessment of their value. At the heart of technical policy disputes are philosophical arguments concerning the relationship between rationality and politics, the definition of what can be done. In modern societies a consensus defines what people can achieve through democratic co-operation and what has to be left to the co-ordination of the price system. The distinction between necessary and unnecessary suffering defines the power of politics to improve the human condition.

---

2. See M.J. Fischer, *Iran: From Religious Dispute to Revolution*, Cambridge Mass. 1980.

3. See chapter six.

4. The reasonable refers to general rules which constrain the pursuit of rational self-interest. See John Rawls, *Political Liberalism*, New York 1993, pp. 148–53. See also Alasdair MacIntyre, *After Virtue: A Study in Moral Theory*, London 1985, p. 23 (hereafter MacIntyre).

Liberal Democracy

The theory of justice defended here upholds the priority of human and civil rights in the constitutional structure of the state.[5] It is argued that justice protects the individual from, among other things, democratic domination. Rights pertain to a sphere of self-directed individual activity which lies outside political negotiation or withdrawal and thus they protect the capacity of the person to live according to internally affirmed commitments. Liberty combines the capacity for freedom with the constraint of negative general laws in the form of individual rights applicable to each person.[6] The establishment of rights is the political means of transforming domination into an association based on a reciprocal recognition of dependency.[7]

Linguistic inheritance, material needs and the skills necessary for their satisfaction demand dependence upon others. The impossibility of individual self-sufficiency does not, however, undermine the justification of individual rights developed here. A shared language, for example, is a precondition of communication, but people can disagree within the same language to the extent that they have waged war on each other for mutually intelligible reasons. The priority of a common language as a necessary condition of thinking does not lead to a privilege for the state in matters of meaning and truth. The possibility of error, the necessity of revision and the diversity of traditions within society mitigate against a communitarian state as the primary site of democracy founded upon the shared patrimony of language alone.

Material needs are also morally arbitrary as they are necessarily unchosen.[8] John Rawls argues that the collective provision of

---

5. In this it is consistent with the conclusions, if not the method, expounded in John Rawls, *A Theory of Justice*, Oxford 1972 (hereafter TOJ).

6. This idea takes the form of the categorical imperative in Kant, the harm principle in Mill or the principle of generative consistency in Gewirth. See I. Kant, 'The Metaphysics of Morals', *Kant's Political Writings*, ed. Hans Riess, Cambridge 1994, pp. 132–5. J.S. Mill, *On Liberty*, London 1984, p. 47. A. Gewirth, *The Principle Of Generative Consistency*, Chicago 1977, p. 14.

7. Domination, the direct coercion of one person or group of persons by the will of another individual or group of individuals, is not a necessary feature of dependence. See Claus Mueller, *The Politics of Communication*, Oxford 1973, p. 129.

8. See Rawls, *Political Liberalism*, pp. 178–95. TOJ, pp. 513–19. See also chapter four.

primary goods, defined as the resources necessary for effectively participating in society, establish a minimal parity between members of society.[9] This equality of status is expressed through the distribution of the necessities of life as well as political freedoms.[10] Welfare, Rawls argues, is a condition of liberty, for it guarantees the personal autonomy necessary for fair terms of social co-operation.[11]

The dilemma for this type of political liberalism is that it is forced to moralize the state in order to justify its expanded welfare role, yet the constraint of neutrality renders democracy a threat to justice.[12] Citizenship defines the nation-state as the supreme collective and moral force while stripping it of all its communal features. The legal and tax systems have to carry the substantial burden of solidarity necessary for sustaining justice. Nonetheless, due to its monopoly of violence, the nation-state remains an inappropriate expression of democratic sovereignty. The possibilities of injustice are permanent and severe if the values of community are conflated with the powers of a collective coercive force.

Democracy, in contrast to rights, is a method of publicly negotiating the distribution of hardship in society and pertains to activities in which co-operation is necessary. Work is a necessity in a material and cultural sense. It is a material necessity, for without the transformation of external nature into humanly created products through active labour, people would starve or freeze. It is a cultural necessity, for without the preservation of the skills, knowledge and the trust required for stable patterns of co-operation, society would be unable to satisfy its needs or co-operate with others to fulfil them.[13] Labour, it will be argued in the next section, is the activity through which people combine their knowledge and energy in order to reproduce their culture and

---

9. See Rawls, *Political Liberalism*, p. 181. TOJ, pp. 258–319. The innovation in the concept of primary goods adopted here is the inclusion of skills, practices and knowledge as necessary conditions of agency.

10. See G.A. Cohen, 'The Structure of Proletarian Unfreedom', *Philosophy and Public Affairs*, Vol. 13, No. 1, 1982.

11. See John Rawls, 'The Basic Liberties and their Priority', in *The Tanner Lectures on Human Values*, Vol. 3, Cambridge 1982. See also Rawls, *Political Liberalism*, pp. 11–35.

12. See Rawls, *Political Liberalism*, pp. 40–3. TOJ, pp. 195–257.

13. See G.W.F. Hegel, *Elements of the Philosophy of Right,* ed. Allen W. Wood, Cambridge 1991. See also his *Jenenser Realphilosophie*, Vol. 2, ed. J. Hoffmeister, Leipzig 1931, p. 214.

satisfy their needs.[14] The communitarian demands of solidarity, courage and loyalty required for durable human association are pluralized through the division of labour and thus do not take the form of statist moralism. Democracy is thus located in the economy.[15] A substantive decentralized democracy is constrained in its oppression through the priority of rights. The compatibility of political rights and economic democracy is effected through their location in the state and the economy respectively. The state upholds individual rights, the organizations of society become the focus of community. Political liberalism is complemented by social democracy.

Karl Polanyi: States, Markets and the Destruction of Society

The substance of society and the commodity fictions

A similar reconciliation of liberty and democracy is developed in the work of Karl Polanyi, who defends two propositions.[16] The first is that each person is constitutively dependent upon a physical environment and other people for the satisfaction of needs. The second is that the economy requires social institutions which disseminate skills, distribute knowledge and preserve the status of human beings and nature as something other than

---

14. For an outstanding analysis of the relationship between culture as an independent factor of analysis and labour as a necessary activity see Richard Biernacki, *The Fabrication of Labour, Germany and Britain 1640–1914*, California 1995.

15. It is easier to change your job than your country.

16. Polanyi wrote only one significant book in his lifetime, *The Great Transformation: The Political and Economic Origins of Our Time*, Boston 1957 (hereafter TGT) [1944]. This has been the principal source for developing the arguments made in this section. Extensive use has also been made of the posthumously published *The Livelihood of Man*, ed. H.W. Pearson, London 1977 (hereafter *Livelihood*). The primary theoretical analysis is developed in 'The Economy as Instituted Process', *Primitive, Archaic and Modern Economies*, ed. George Dalton, Boston 1968, pp. 139–74 (hereafter 'Instituted Process'). Giovanni Arrighi's *The Long Twentieth Century: Money, Power and the Origins of Our Time* (hereafter Arrighi) London 1995, develops many of Polanyi's ideas and is incorporated into this section.

commodities.[17] Societal institutions protect the cultural resources of society from depletion and exhaustion by regulating production and educating the person. Polanyi's central contention is that a market economy is based on three 'commodity fictions', labour, land and money, which as they are not produced for sale are not commodities at all. In a market society, however, the raw material of factor markets becomes indistinguishable from the three elements which, he claims, form the 'substance of society': 'human beings, their natural surroundings and productive organizations'.[18] Land and labour are alternative descriptions of nature and human beings.[19]

Labour, Polanyi argues, is not a commodity as people are not produced for sale.[20] It is also an activity inseparable from the body and life of a person and cannot, therefore, be stored up or reinvested. As work is a necessary activity, the institutions of its reproduction are constitutive of society.[21] The second commodity fiction of land is 'only another word for nature and is . . . inextricably interwoven with man's institutions'.[22] Land is inherited and not produced, it is a gift of geography and history.[23] The safety of food production and environmental reproduction are threatened by an exclusive reliance on the market mechanism. Money, the third commodity fiction, is produced by the state as a token of exchange and not as a saleable commodity.[24]

Polanyi's theory of history

The historical narrative developed by Karl Polanyi in *The Great Transformation* is that as society develops in size, technological power and complexity, it tends to be eliminated by the centralized

---

17. Commodities are defined as objects produced for sale on the open market. Commodification takes place when that which was previously regulated, organized or distributed by institutions becomes available only through market exchange. TGT, p. 72.

18. TGT, p. 162.

19. TGT, p. 71.

20. *Livelihood*, p. 10.

21. 'The organisation of labour is only another term for the forms of life of the common people'. TGT, p. 75.

22. TGT, pp. 178, 72.

23. TGT, p. 69.

24. TGT, p. 195.

state and the competitive economy. The emerging nation-state subordinates the existing institutions of social organization, such as cities, guilds, corporations, churches, unions, parishes, municipalities and estates, by establishing unmediated sovereignty, a national currency and uniformity of tariffs within its borders. The market, in its turn, opens up the substance of society for sale on the open market. Confronted by stable patterns of production characterized by quality control and apprenticeships with their strict barriers to entry, the market solution is to abolish co-operation. Society, understood as a stable network of self-governing institutions as well as self-regulating systems, disintegrates.

The link between atomism and nationalism, Polanyi argues, is forged by their mutual contempt for societal institutions and traditions. An individualistic internal order is complemented by an anarchistic global order with sovereignty uniting the two domains.[25] Both the sovereign agent of rational choice and the sovereign state of politics view dependency as a weakness, a denial of autonomy, and are constantly resisting the demands of social and economic co-operation brought about by the division of labour and the intensification of dependency this brings. Those autonomous societal institutions which organize the satisfaction of need and the preservation of a practical culture are considered a constraint on the individual freedoms of the person and the political will of the state. Squeezed between the individual maximizer and the collective aggregator, society as a functional moral entity disappears.

Polanyi claims that while the idea of the economy as a self-regulating system of exchange grounded in individual choice, governed by prices and constrained by scarcity becomes dominant, it is based on an impoverished conception of the importance of the economy and its institutions in the reproduction of ethics and society.[26] The extension of the formal conception from the market to all the economic institutions of society is what Polanyi calls 'market utopianism'.[27] This conception of economics simultaneously seals off the economy from social institutions and political interference in the name of self-regulation and individual

---

25. TGT, p. 253.
26. For the distinction between the substantive and formal meanings of economic, see 'Instituted Process' and *Livelihood*, p. xlvi.
27. TGT, p. 42.

sovereignty while expanding the domain of its analysis to include all elements of culture as conforming with the motivation of rational self-interest. The substantive institutions necessary for the material satisfaction of wants and the preservation of skills are abolished as archaic constraints on trade and interferences with liberty. The market becomes a self-fulfilling fallacy as the power of the state is used to define all conceptions of rationality or agency which do not conform to the principle of interest maximization as irrational and illegal. 'The road to the free market was opened and kept open by an enormous increase in continuous centrally organized and controlled interventionism.'[28]

States and markets are thus mutually necessary at the initial stage of state-building as regards uniformity of taxes, tariffs and the free mobility of labour and capital within a sovereign territory.[29] States and markets are also self-generating in that the breaking of society, its patterns of work and local modes of association leads to the emergence of two dominating and potentially irreconcilable institutions: the market as the principle of dynamism and the state as the representative of generalized community. Unmediated dependence on the market for wages leads logically to an unmediated dependency on the state as the protector of community. Having initially been the necessary condition for creating a market economy, the state subsequently takes on a welfare role. The political rationality of nationalism is that it presented a way in which society could resist the claims of the market. The plural institutions of society could only do so, however, by becoming increasingly dependent on the state.[30] Localized forms of resistance are forced to make national alliances in order to survive.[31] It is the eradication of the reciprocity embodied in autonomous and decentralized societal institutions that leads to the domination of markets and states.

The contradiction between the commodity fictions and the

---

28. TGT, p. 140.

29. For an account of how the British state used its power to undermine guild structures see J.R. Kellett, 'The Breakdown of Gild and Corporation Control over the Handicraft and Retail Trade of London', *Economic History Review*, Vol. 10, No. 3, 1958.

30. For the growth of national unions as a response to local ineffectiveness see J. Zeitlin, 'From Labour History to the History of Industrial Relations', *Economic History Review*, Vol. 40, No. 2, 1987, pp. 159–84.

31. *Livelihood*, p. l.

substance of society is the central explanatory postulate in Polanyi's theory.[32] This derives, he argues, from two incompatible meanings of the word economic, one formal, the other substantive.[33] The formal meaning refers to the rational calculation of means to ends under conditions of scarcity. Rationality consists of a set of rules which determine the choice between alternative uses of insufficient means in order to maximize returns. This describes the activity of economizing, defined as the greatest frugality of expenditure in the securing of ends. The substantive definition of the economy concerns the material satisfaction of needs through practices which organize the dependencies upon other people and the environment required in securing one's livelihood.[34] The human being survives, Polanyi argues, 'by virtue of an institutionalized relationship' between nature and society.[35] The 'economistic fallacy' is based upon the conflation of a mental process of calculation with the substantive practices of production. The imposition of a formal model on a society eliminates ethics from the economy, institutions from the organization of production, and any motivation other than self-interest from the domain of rationality.[36] This has a deleterious effect on the capacity of individuals in society to co-operate in the reciprocal satisfaction of wants and needs.

The rate of change

The key term in any transformation is the rate of change which, Polanyi argues, is as important as its direction.[37] This is the result of the conflict between tradition and innovation, and expresses itself in the delaying tactics and resistances that allow a society to preserve its meanings and practices when confronted by changes in the external environment which require institutional adaptation.[38] If improvement demands too great a social dislocation, society disintegrates. Each significant transformation is characterized by a 'storm' during which the 'substance' of society is imperilled.

---

32. TGT, p. 33.
33. 'Instituted Process', pp. 146–56. *Livelihood*, pp. 5–34.
34. 'Instituted Process', p. 148.
35. *Livelihood*, pp. 5–8.
36. *Livelihood*, p. 11.
37. TGT, pp. 35–7.
38. TGT, p. 35.

9

Polanyi gives three examples of significant technological and ideological change in which the organizations of society were threatened by the commodification of culture: enclosures, industrialization and the collapse of the gold standard.

Tudor labour laws

Polanyi's first analysis of the rate of change is his appreciation of Tudor and early Stuart policy of using the power of the crown to slow down the societal disintegration caused by enclosures.[39] He argues that the monarchy and Church defended 'the human and natural substance of society' from the effects of the privatization of the common lands which were: 'wasting its towns, decimating its population, turning its over-burdened soil into dust, harassing its people and turning them from decent husbandmen into a mob of beggars and thieves'.[40]

The principle means of doing this was through the Poor Law of 1601 and the national enforcement of the Statute of Artificers of 1563. This required seven-year apprenticeships, yearly wage assessments and the national enforcement of labour statutes.[41] Britain became the first country in Europe to enforce national institutions of labour protection and quality control.[42] The extension of guild regulation concentrated resources on armaments and luxury goods through the improvements effected in new techniques. From a relatively backward position in all areas except the production of tin and pewter, by the seventeenth century British cannon were in demand throughout the continent and a competitive advantage was established in silk, glass and the manufacture of fine paper.[43] The shift from cloth to luxury goods and armaments effected through the state recognition of the role of vocational organization in the workplace, led to the competitive

---

39. See J.R. Wordie, 'The Chronology of English Enclosure, 1500–1914', *Economic History Review*, Second Series, 1983. TGT, pp. 35–7.
40. TGT, p. 35.
41. TGT, p. 70.
42. TGT, p. 303.
43. See John U. Nef, 'The Progress of Technology and the Growth of Large-Scale Industry in Great Britain, 1560–1640', *Economic History Review*, Vol. 5, No. 1, 1934, pp. 3–24. Christopher Hill, *Reformation to Industrial Revolution: A Social and Economic History of Britain, 1530–1780*, London 1967, pp. 63–75. Also Arrighi, pp. 183–95.

'breakthrough in high value added activities' characteristic of early British industrialization.[44] The direction of change towards a land market was maintained, its rate was slowed. In this way the 'fabric' of society was re-woven without being rent.

Speenhamland

Polanyi's second example of the rate of change is his analysis of the Speenhamland scale that characterized British welfare policy between 1795 and 1834.

> The justices of Berkshire, meeting at the Pelikan Inn, in Speenhamland, near Newbury, on May 6, 1795, in a time of great distress, decided that subsidies in aid of wages should be granted in accordance with a scale dependent on the price of bread, so that a minimum income should be assured to the poor irrespective of their earnings.[45]

Superficially, Speenhamland appears as a means by which society resists the claims of the market through the introduction of a basic income, or 'right to live'.[46] It was the eighteenth-century equivalent of the citizen's wage in which each subject was given an unconditional payment sufficient for the satisfaction of needs.[47] The fatality of Speenhamland, argues Polanyi, was that by outlawing the guilds as organizations that taught and reproduced skills, it destroyed standards of work through severing the link with quality maintained by apprenticeships and wages.[48] The repeal of the apprenticeship clauses of the Elizabethan Statute of Artificers in 1814 meant that knowledge and skills were no longer considered protected property.[49] Through the withdrawal of status, confiscation of land and the breakdown of reciprocal dependency on others, the labourer became dependent on either the market for

---

44. Arrighi, p. 195.
45. TGT, p. 78.
46. TGT, p. 165.
47. For recent defences of this policy see Phillipe Van Parijs, ed., *Arguing for Basic Income*, London 1992.
48. The anti-combination laws of 1799–1800 made worker association a criminal offence.
49. See T.K. Derry, 'The Repeal of the Apprenticeship Clauses of the Statutes of Apprenticeship', *Economic History Review*, Vol. 3, 1931, pp. 67–87. See also David McNally, *Against the Market: Political Economy, Market Socialism and the Marxist Critique*, London 1993, pp. 34–42.

wages or the state for outdoor relief.[50] The reduction of the person to a dependent pauper deprived of responsibility and recognition was, argues Polanyi, 'the supreme abomination of Speenhamland'.[51] Its effects were such that the most persuasive moral argument for the establishment of a free market in land and labour was that welfare destroyed the virtues necessary for the survival of society. In the organization of the economy, ethics was abolished as injurious to the common good. 'Fear of starvation with the worker and lure of profit with the employer' became the motivational assumptions of society.[52]

The unity of the new discipline of political economy as defined in Joseph Townsend's *Dissertation on the Poor Laws*, Ricardo's *Principles of Political Economy and Taxation* and Malthus's *Essay on the Principle of Population*, was given by their common argument that the right to life undermined the vitality of society.[53] The application of 'nature's penalty' of hunger was considered the most effective means of securing the satisfaction of needs. While Hobbes argued that men behaved like beasts, Townsend argued that similes were superfluous.[54] A biological foundation was found for the political order.[55] The body politic was replaced by the demands of the body itself, and the imperatives of biological survival defined the new 'law of nature'.[56] Malthus did not doubt the intensity of grief caused by the establishment of starvation-driven incentives but it was necessary suffering. The distribution of poverty was not amenable to public intervention. The abolition of the Poor

---

50. The Black Acts of 1793 further criminalized customary practice such as fruit picking and cutting wood. See John Rule, *The Experience of Labour in Eighteenth Century Industry*, London 1981, pp. 124–33. See also C.R. Dobson. *Masters and Journeymen: A Prehistory of Industrial Relations 1717–1800*, London 1980, pp. 27–9.

51. TGT, p. 99.

52. *Livelihood*, p. 11.

53. Joseph Townsend, *Dissertation on the Poor Laws*, London 1776. Thomas R. Malthus, *An Essay on the Principle of Population*, ed. Donald Winch, Cambridge 1992 [1798]. David Ricardo, *On the Principles of Political Economy and Taxation*, ed. Piero Sraffa and M.H. Dobb, Cambridge 1951.

54. TGT, p. 113.

55. Ricardo, in Polanyi's words, conceived of the labour market as 'a flow of human lives the supply of which was regulated by the amount of food put at their disposal'. TGT, p. 164.

56. See M. Young, 'Malthus and the Evolutionists: The Common Context of Biological and Social Theory', *Past and Present*, No. 43, 1969, p. 119.

Law and the commons meant that those who wished to serve could find food while the poor:

> should be taught to know that the laws of nature, which are the laws of God, had doomed him and his family to starve . . . They have no claim of right on society for the smallest portion of food, beyond that which their labour could fairly purchase; and that if he and his family were saved from suffering the utmost extremities of hunger, he would owe it to the pity of some kind benefactor, to whom, therefore, he would be tied by the strongest ties of gratitude.[57]

The causes of poverty could only be overcome through the imposition of new incentive structures. The Poor Law Amendment Act of 1834 established the first free market in labour.[58] Aid in wages and outdoor relief were abolished. The Bank Act of 1834 subordinated the domestic economy to the gold standard and the Anti-Corn Law Bill of the same year established a free market in agriculture. A market society replaced the market economy. Man and nature became commodities in the form of rent and wages and their survival dependent on the money system. Speenhamland eroded the status of worker, market utopianism abolished the status of the person. The result was that: 'An avalanche of social dislocation, surpassing by far that of the enclosure period, came down upon England'.[59]

The cause of the eventual antagonism between markets and states is to be found in the tension between the logic of a self-regulating market encompassing all elements of industry and the demands of societal survival. While the form of resistance to the commodification of labour and land differed, the substance of the threat was shared.[60] Factory Acts and compulsory schools, fire brigades and municipal libraries, public parks and agricultural

---

57. Malthus, p. 263. In the 1806 edition the word 'starve' was replaced by 'suffer'.

58. The defeat of Fielden's Bill in 1835, which tried to set a national rate for the handloom weavers, was repeated for the next six years. See Paul Richards, 'The State and Early Industrial Capital: The Case of the Handloom Weavers', *Past and Present*, No. 83, 1979, pp. 91–115.

59. TGT, p. 40.

60. TGT, p. 130. While it is central to Polanyi's argument that culture played an independent role in shaping the response of each society to threats to its survival, the elements of a culture (land, labour and knowledge) are necessary features of all societies. See Biernacki, *The Fabrication of Labour,* chapters one and two.

protection, fixed rates and factory inspections emerged as the substantive subject matter of politics throughout Europe.[61] The spread of international markets was combined with the protection of the elements of a culture. Polanyi argues that while 'Laissez-Faire was enforced by the state, resistance was spontaneous'.[62] Victorian England and Bismarck's Prussia were as different from each other as the Hapsburg Empire or the French Third Republic. Each passed from a period of market utopianism to the state-enforced protection of the value of land, labour and money from the demands of market sovereignty after 1875.[63]

The distinction between the formal and substantive conception of the economy provides Polanyi with his theory of historical agency. Resistance to the imposition of the formal model will cluster, he argues, around the substantive elements of a culture, labour and land.[64] Peasants' parties, socialist or Catholic workers' movements and aristocratic families defended a status for human beings and nature which did not take a commodity form and provided the social basis of state power throughout industrialization.[65] During the last third of the nineteenth century society succeeded, in different ways and with different alliances, to disentangle real commodities from fictitious ones.[66] Markets in finished goods expanded, markets in labour, land and money were constrained. The fabric of society was protected from the fabrication of labour. Health, housing, work safety and social insurance were included in the definition of statecraft.

The inter-war years

The sequence of market utopianism followed by communitarian statism characteristic of the late nineteenth century was repeated at a more intense level during the third 'storm' of commodification of the inter-war years. The 1920s saw a resurgence of market utopianism in which:

---

61. See chapter three, pp. 70–79 and chapter two, pp. 43–50.
62. TGT, p. 139.
63. See George Steinmetz, *Regulating the Social: The Welfare State and Local Politics in Imperial Germany*, Princeton 1993.
64. TGT, p. 183.
65. Disraeli founded the Conservative Party in opposition to the New Poor Law of 1834. The role of the Catholic Church and the labour movement in Germany is developed in the next chapter. TGT, pp. 185–9.
66. See Arrighi, p. 267.

The stabilization of the currency became the focal point in the political thoughts of peoples and governments; the restoration of the gold standard became the supreme aim of all organized effort in the economic field.[67]

In a monetized economy the value of a currency becomes a vital determinant in the satisfaction of needs. The protection of the currency thus became the prime responsibility of the state and led to the subordination of politics to the demands of financial orthodoxy in order to protect purchasing power.[68] Under these conditions people's sustenance, employment and accommodation become dependent on the value of a currency.[69] The irony of national sovereignty is that its attainment led directly to financial subordination within the international economic system. Measures taken by the state to relieve the resulting unemployment and social dislocation were punished by the constraint of capital flight and currency collapse. In Austria in 1923, Belgium and France in 1926, Germany in 1931 and Great Britain in 1933, Labour parties had to resign from office for the sake of a stable currency. The policies pursued by Brüning's administration in the Weimar Republic, in which centralized fiscal orthodoxy was pursued as a means of undermining both vocational and regional autonomy and the replacement of parliamentary decision by administrative directives, were, Polanyi argues, a necessary condition for the abolition of the Republic in 1933.[70]

Each country, whether it was New Deal America or the Soviet Union, Nazi Germany or welfarist Britain, responded to the threat that market economies posed to the existence of society by releasing labour, land and money from subordination to the price system alone.[71] Employment provision, industrial intervention, agricultural protection, the setting of currency rates and the provision of basic needs outside the market system became the responsibility of

---

67. TGT, p. 142.
68. See Arrighi, p. 73.
69. TGT, pp. 24–7.
70. For Brüning's use of currency reform as a means of centralizing state power see Hans Mommsen, *From Weimar to Auschwitz*, Cambridge 1992, p. 127. For the emergence of government by direction as a means of bypassing parliament see pp. 132–5. For the disregard for the constitution see p. 140. TGT, p. 229. Also see chapter two, pp. 43–50.
71. TGT, pp. 249, 76. See also p. 142.

government in each of these regimes. Intervention was invariably undertaken in order to strengthen 'social security' through regulating the labour market, assuring continuity of production, protecting land from commodification and enforcing the value of the currency.

The reasons Polanyi gives for the emergence of Fascism are that, through the pursuit of currency convertibility, sovereign states were politically debarred from intervening in the economy so as to alleviate suffering or prevent ethical disintegration. 'Questions of social organization had to be wholly subordinated to the need of the restoration of currency.'[72] Liberty came to be identified with poverty. Any form of resistance to the utopia of a society governed only by prices and contract was defined as impractical and immoral. If markets are understood as uncoerced spontaneous outcomes unamenable to intervention, the role of politics is definitively subordinate.[73] The priority of fiscal policy generated 'a decisive weakening of the democratic forces which might have otherwise averted a fascist catastrophe'.[74] 'The victory of fascism was made practically unavoidable by the liberals' obstruction of any reform involving planning, regulation or control.'[75] Polanyi's explanation of the savagery characteristic of the first half of the twentieth century is primarily conceptual and boils down to the thesis that once economic rationality and 'reasons of state' become severed from the institutions of society, the trust, skills and solidarity necessary for its survival disintegrate.[76] Disembedded rationality and disembodied polities lead to a vacillation between the state as the defender of order and the market as the sphere of freedom.

The dilemma which confronted market societies was that the virtue required for sustainable association was transferred from the non-pecuniary decentralized institutions which were previously entangled in the economy such as the guilds, the Church and the city and came to be located in the state as the only force capable of resisting the claims of the market. The state, however, was

---

72. TGT, p. 237.
73. 'The triumph of economic rationalism', wrote Polanyi, was 'the eclipse of political thought'. *Livelihood*, p. 14.
74. TGT, p. 148.
75. TGT, p. 257.
76. TGT, p. 249.

incapable of fulfilling its role as the representative and organizer of a complex society. Through an excessive reliance on centralized redistribution and directives, it further broke immediate practices of reciprocity. If the economistic fallacy consists of equating the human economy with its market form, then the nationalistic fallacy lay in conflating society and the state. Against these two abstractions Polanyi proposes the idea of a substantive society.

Reciprocity, redistribution and exchange: the priority of society

Polanyi is not making an argument for the elimination of markets or for state planning.[77] The state is necessary as the guarantor of justice, regulation and recognition; the market as the uncoerced sphere of exchange. A substantive economy, however, requires a society based upon non-market institutions which plays a role in the provision of needs, the distribution of knowledge and the allocation of status. 'The human economy', Polanyi writes, 'is embedded and enmeshed in institutions, economic and non-economic' which are fundamental to the preservation of reciprocity as the prevailing 'pattern of interaction' within the economy.[78]

The 'form of integration' pertaining in society refers to the different spheres in which reciprocity, redistribution and exchange are the dominant principles of social organization. Exchange describes uncoerced transactions between agents resulting in a re-appropriation of title. Redistribution designates a transfer of goods to the centre and their subsequent reallocation. Reciprocity describes exchanges between people or groups which do not take on the form of either self-interest or obligation. Each sphere requires distinct institutional arrangements: exchange a price-making system, redistribution a central organization, and reciprocity the distinct institutions and practices which preserve patterns of non-contractual solidarity.

The demand for reciprocity is greatest in the productive economy as the dependency is threefold. There is a direct interaction with the environment, an immediate dependency on the effective manipulation of technology and, therefore, upon others for the

77. This point is well made in Christopher M. Hahn, 'Radical Functionalism: The Life and Work of Karl Polanyi', *Dialectical Anthropology*, Vol. 17, 1992, pp. 141–66.
78. 'Instituted Process', p. 148.

17

appropriate fulfilment of their tasks. The means through which the solidarity necessary for survival is maintained requires the subordination of the joint sovereignty of exchange and redistribution to autonomous societal institutions. Redistribution, as a statist principle, denies the reciprocal dependencies and decentralized diversity that characterize complex systems of economic co-operation. Market exchange, in its turn, necessarily ignores the role of supply-side institutions which regulate the valorized supply of skilled persons. Public goods require constraints on individual interest maximization and the avoidance of state direction.[79] Redistribution and exchange are institutional practices that have characterized the broadest range of economies. Reciprocity is destroyed, however, if either the state or the market dominate the 'patterns of association' which constitute society.

Economies thus require institutions with a non-pecuniary rationality which foster reciprocity as well as exchange and redistribution. In a market society the institutions which sustain the virtue necessary for the fulfilment of common tasks are deemed to be a constraint on freedom and the provision of welfare inimical to the survival of society. Market relations, however, break down if they are not constrained by forces which protect the status of nature and the person from 'degeneration' and exhaustion. Polanyi's paradoxical conclusion is that in terms of economic theory, 'pre-modern' vocational institutions are a precondition of sustaining competitive productive practices.

If the traditional institutions of a society are either outlawed or excluded from the moulding of a transformation, then there are no agents in society capable of sustaining a productive relationship with the challenges posed by change. A breakdown occurs in which: 'The new economic institutions fail to be assimilated by the native culture which consequently disintegrates without being replaced by any other coherent value system.'[80] There is no constructive medium of constraint and facilitation. As it changes form, society dissolves. A social calamity is ultimately a cultural not an economic phenomenon. Unmediated dependency on either the state for welfare or the market for wages breaks the institutional

---

79. See next section.
80. TGT, p. 291.

status of tradition, defined as the practices necessary for durable forms of association. This takes place through 'the lethal injuries to the institutions in which social existence is embedded which result in the loss of self-respect and standards'.[81] Existing social organizations adapt to the challenges posed to their existence by universal markets and generalized states by maintaining the 'shape' of human association while assimilating the changes necessary to renew production methods.[82]

Institutions secure the continuous satisfaction of needs by rendering reliable the human dependency necessary in order to reproduce the conditions of continued life. Traditions have a double function. They are what Polanyi calls a 'medium' that orders and absorbs the social dislocation that results from societal transformation.[83] Functionally, institutions control the dislocation generated during the period of adaptation to the demands of new technologies, administrative techniques and practical rules. Traditions are also an active means of assimilation. They preserve the patterns of reciprocity which translate external dangers and possibilities into a communicable language of skills and practices.[84] This facilitates a comprehensible adaptation to a changed environment. Institutions thus secure the supply of skill and reliability necessary for the survival of society. This is Polanyi's point when he claims that institutions 'are embodiments of human meaning and purpose'.[85] The next section is a development of these ideas, most particularly the role of economic institutions in disseminating knowledge, preserving ethics and satisfying need.

The Virtue Economy

The argument presented in this section is that through the public recognition of institutions which preserve and teach the practices of specialized disciplines, defined by their own internal goods of quality and expertise, the capacity of the economy to innovate

---

81. TGT, p. 130.
82. This, it will be argued in chapter three, is the case with the artisan sector of the German economy.
83. TGT p. 98. See also MacIntyre, p. 194.
84. TGT, p. 83.
85. TGT, p. 254.

and adapt to changes in their environment is enhanced.[86] The scope of these non-market institutions ranges from universities through artisan organizations to self-regulated professions such as law and medicine.[87] Each serves as a source of moral regulation and expertise in the economy, particularly concerning the valorized supply of labour and the enforcement of quality control. The culture formed by these public institutions generates trust as a reasonable expectation. This type of reciprocity is necessary in economies characterized by exacting methods of production and is undermined by an exclusive reliance on individual self-interest in the organization of economic co-operation.[88] Sustainable economic activity presupposes a society characterized by robust non-market institutions entangled within the economy which are best described as vocational. Vocational organizations are based upon the preservation of institutional authority within the economy through the granting of work licences which permit the practice of a trade through the fulfilment of an apprenticeship. It is only with the approval of recognized and self-organized institutions that a person may participate in their chosen sector of activity.

The argument presented here is that economic virtue, based on the development of justice, honesty, solidarity and courage in the organization of working practices, is a necessary condition of interna-

---

86. The analysis developed in this section has been greatly helped by the article by Mark Elam, 'Markets, Morals and the Powers of Innovation', *Economy and Society*, Vol. 22, No. 1, 1993, pp. 1–41 (hereafter Elam). Also of great importance were Zeitlin, 'From Labour History to the History of Industrial Relations'; Arndt Sorge and Wolfgang Streeck, 'Industrial Relations and Technical Change: The Case for an Extended Perspective', in R. Hyman and W. Streeck, eds, *New Technology and Industrial Relations*, Oxford 1988, pp. 19–47; Charles Sabel and Jonathan Zeitlin, 'Historical Alternatives to Mass Production: Politics, Markets and Technology in Nineteenth Century Industrialisation', *Past and Present*, No. 108, 1985, pp. 133–76 (hereafter 'Historical Alternatives'); Paul Hirst and Jonathan Zeitlin, 'Flexible Specialisation versus Post-Fordism: Theory, Evidence and Policy Implications', *Economy and Society*, Vol. 20, No. 1, 1991, pp. 1–56; Wolfgang Streeck, 'Productive Constraints: On the Institutional Conditions of Diversified Quality Production', in *Social Institutions and Economic Performance: Studies of Industrial Relations in Advanced Capitalist Economies*, London 1992, pp. 1–40.

87. The link between virtue and education has been developed most extensively by Alasdair MacIntyre who defines virtue as: 'an acquired human quality the possession and exercise of which tends to enable us to achieve those goods which are internal to practices and the lack of which effectively prevents us from achieving any such goods'. MacIntyre, *After Virtue*, p. 191.

88. Hirst, 'Flexible Specialisation', p. 7.

tional competitive success in modern manufacture. Such economies have a greater chance of flourishing than those based on the imperative of immediate returns on investment and a strict enforcement of managerial prerogative.[89] It is on the basis of existing knowledge that the changes resulting from innovation can be assimilated.[90] Technology can only function if there is enough expertise existing within the firm to repair, retool, redesign and reset it.[91] The neo-classical institutional minimum of managerial prerogative and competitive markets seals off the workshop from decision making. The point of production, however, is where quality is built into the product.

> All the information inscribed in textbooks, journals, reports, databases, patents, blueprints, standards, instruction manuals and so on, is just so much 'empty talk' unless it is brought to life and lived in and out by skilled individuals.[92]

Each firm has a fund of knowledge dispersed among its workers. The demands of a changing environment require a collective response from the firm. The exclusion of those who operate at the point of production from the process of adaptation hinders the technological innovation necessary for effective adjustment.[93] New patterns of productivity are based on greater 'workflow integration' organized around the swift capacity to vary the settings and design of a product for specific batches of production.[94] This is achieved by redistributing authority to the workplace.[95] Work ethics, as with any other kind of ethical practice, require institutions which preserve and disseminate the necessary practices.

---

89. See Streeck, 'Productive Constraints', p. 4.

90. See G. Dosi, 'Sources, Procedures and Microeconomic Effects of Innovation' *Journal of Economic Literature*, Vol. 26, 1988, pp. 1120–71. Innovation is the capacity to reorder received ideas and practices rather than engage in creative construction from first principles.

91. See Elam, p. 9. Streeck, 'Productive Constraints', pp. 15–20, and Hirst, 'Flexible Specialisation', p. 42.

92. Elam, p. 3.

93. See W. Lazonik, *Competitive Advantage on the Shop Floor*, Cambridge Mass. 1990, chapters nine and ten.

94. Sorge, 'Industrial Relations', pp. 25–8.

95. The works councils within the German economy continually encouraged and protected vocational training, re-training and task enlargement. See Sorge, 'Industrial Relations', pp. 23–5. Elam, p. 28. For a more abstract discussion see M. Aoki, 'Horizontal versus vertical information structure of the firm', *American Economic Review*, Vol. 76, 1986, pp. 971–83.

The good society and the production of goods

A good society, defined as a society capable of producing goods, requires the capacity to curtail greed through public constraints which punish corruption and free-riding.[96] This, in turn, requires institutions of moral regulation within the economy that preserve the skills and practices required for concerted responses to innovation and uncertainty.[97] Vocational institutions preserve the practices of virtue within the culture of production and this demands constraints on individual self-interest. Of necessity these come to take a civic form.[98]

German industry, for example, benefits from a strong artisan sector.[99] Without legislation that forbade industrial firms from entering the artisanal domain, their fate would have been the same as the former craftsmen of Britain.[100] Strict protection of trade, the enforcement of vocational qualifications and decentralized quality control preserved artisan skills. These constraints on individual economic freedom were of considerable advantage to large German firms as changes in demand and the technological elimination of routine jobs required higher quality workers and greater co-operation and dependence at the workplace.[101]

Under such a regime, the locality and district in the form of cities and municipalities become entangled in the process of production. Non-market institutions participate in the economy as

---

96. To paraphrase Machiavelli, rational agents must learn when not to be rational. See N. Machiavelli, *The Prince*, ed. Q. Skinner and R. Price, Cambridge 1994, pp. 88–90.

97. For a selection of essays which clarify many of the concepts used in this section see J.C. Nyiri and Barry Smith, eds, *Practical Knowledge: Outlines of a Theory of Tradition and Skills*, London 1988. See also Stephen Turner, *The Social Theory of Practices: Tradition, Tacit Knowledge and Presuppositions*, Chicago 1994.

98. See Wolfgang Streeck, 'Beneficial Constraints: On the Economic Limits of Rational Voluntarism' Conference Paper, New York 1993, p. 2.

99. See chapter three, pp. 70–9.

100. See C. Lane, 'Industrial Change in Europe: The Pursuit of Flexible Specialisation in Britain and West-Germany', *Work Employment and Society*, Vol. 12, No. 2, 1988, pp. 141–68. See also A. Doran, *Craft Enterprises in Britain and Germany: A Sectoral Study*, London 1984.

101. See S. Brusco and C. Sabel, 'Artisanal Production and Economic Growth' in F. Wilkinson, ed., *The Dynamics of Labour Market Segmentation*, London 1981, pp. 99–114.

active agents.[102] Through the preservation of non-instrumental institutions that uphold values other than exclusively competitive advantage, an ethos of production is preserved which as a public good bestows a considerable competitive advantage in open markets.[103] By regulating the supply side in fictitious commodities, the demand for real commodities is capable of fulfilment.

It was the lack of successful penetration by market methods in the formation of labour markets that bequeathed a comparative advantage to certain regions in developing new methods of large-scale production of customized goods. Recent research corroborates Polanyi's argument that supposedly pre-modern work practices enhance competitiveness.[104]

> In West-Germany and Italy flexible specialization has been based on legacies of labour skill and institutions of regional and social co-operation that persisted into the supposedly 'Fordist' era . . . Social continuity has provided the stability and support to absorb and promote radical change in technology and economic organization.[105]

What Hirst and Zeitlin refer to as 'flexible specialization', what Streeck calls 'diversified quality production', and what is described here as the virtue economy, requires an 'irreducible minimum of trust and co-operation' between agents.[106] This involves constraints on certain types of competition such as sweatshop labour as a public 'bad'. The national setting of wage rates, the vocational administration of training, factory-level democracy and legitimate procedures of arbitration are characteristic of substantive economies.[107] A dense local and vocational network of institutions

---

102. For the importance of industrial districts see Hirst, 'Flexible Specialisation' pp. 3–4 and pp. 42–3. Among the public goods supplied by the region are training, research, market forecasting, credit and quality control. One of the most important functions of regions is to 'take wages out of competition and maintain welfare services in order to avoid debilitating breakdowns of solidarity among economic actors'. Hirst, p. 5.

103. See Hirst, 'Flexible Specialisation' p. 44. This parallels the Tudor use of apprenticeships and the increase in high value added competitive advantage that ensued. See chapter one, pp. 5–19.

104. See particularly Zeitlin, 'From Labour History to the History of Industrial Relations'.

105. Hirst, 'Flexible Specialisation', pp. 11–12.

106. Hirst, 'Flexible Specialisation', p. 7.

107. These are present, for example, in Baden Württemberg, North Rhine

which regulate the productive process flourishes in defiance of the prevailing regime of economic rationality.

There is thus a tension in contemporary economies between the formal pattern of ownership and substantive patterns of production. On the one hand, there is an increase in the importance of specialized co-operation in the preservation of economic capacity. On the other, there is an imposition of individual property rights in the allocation of reward and the distribution of authority within the firm. The application of formal economic models, however, conceals the practices of sustainable production. This tension could be described as a conflict between the forces and the relations of knowledge. The forces of knowledge are based on intellectual copyright, managerial prerogative and competitive markets. The relations of knowledge are characterized by the pooling and sharing of information between and within firms, the institutional participation of work-based organizations in the management of the enterprise and the provision of vocational training. If an information regime is imposed that prohibits the provision of public goods and conceives of vocational practices as an unfair restraint on trade, then the productive capacity of the economy is threatened.

Hayek: the rationality of tradition

What is at stake is best appreciated by a brief analysis of F.A. Hayek's thesis concerning information and economic innovation. Hayek's argument is based upon the limits of rationality. In opposing what he defined as 'constructivist rationalism' he assumed an undesigned or 'spontaneous' order generated by the actions of agents who are necessarily ignorant and operate under conditions which are constitutively uncertain. Within the constraints of general rules based upon rights and an unfettered price system, human beings co-ordinate their actions with such intense density and complexity that no mind or machine could simulate its workings or duplicate its function. The discovery process of the market, Hayek

Westphalia, Veneto and Emilia, all of which are examples of successful manufacturing regions with strong municipal roles in the supply of information, the training of labour and the protection of skill. For Italy see S. Brusco, 'The Emilian Model: Productive Decentralisation and Social Integration', *Cambridge Journal of Economics*, Vol. 6, No. 2, 1982, pp. 167–84.

argues, is based on the necessity of error.[108] Revision can only be protected through the generalized rules which 'assure the individual of the right within a known domain to pursue his own aims on the basis of his own knowledge'.[109]

Socialism, Hayek argued, combined the twin fallacies of hyper-rationalism in its administration and atavistic communitarianism in those matters concerning ethics and moral argument. Collective bureaucratic procedure was combined with a singular and intimate notion of community.[110] Socialism as a form of statistical communitarianism was based on erroneous scientific claims concerning the possibilities of human reason to tame uncertainty through the procedure of collective calculation. Social justice is meaningless, he argues, for it presupposes the 'anthropomorphic fallacy' of a responsible, thinking, rational organization called society.[111] In contrast, society is a huge evolving experiment in which generalized ignorance is mitigated by decentralized decisions, the unintended consequence of which is an order based on abstract rules which uphold the autonomy of the individual.[112] Hayek writes: 'Like all abstractions, justice is an adaptation to our ignorance – to our permanent ignorance of particular facts which no scientific advance can wholly remove.'[113] Individual property rights are thus a precondition of effective economic co-operation.

The central concept in Hayek's epistemology is that of tradition, defined as the subordination of desires to learnt rules. He writes that: 'Custom and tradition stand between instinct and reason . . . without particular traditions the extended order of existence could not continue to exist.'[114] Knowing how is different

---

108. See F.A. Hayek, *Law, Legislation and Liberty, Vol. 3: The Political Order of a Free People*, London 1979, p. 96 (hereafter LLL3).

109. LLL3, p. 130.

110. LLL3. p. 169 in which socialism is defined as 'reactionary' and dependent upon the 'revival of primordial instincts'. See also F.A. Hayek, *Knowledge, Evolution and Society*, London 1983, p. 41.

111. LLL3, p. 136.

112. F.A. Hayek, *The Fatal Conceit: The Errors of Socialism*, London 1988, pp. 7–8 (hereafter *Errors*).

113. F.A. Hayek, *Law, Legislation and Liberty Vol. 2: The Mirage of Social Justice*, London 1976, p. 39 (hereafter LLL2). See also F.A. Hayek, *Law Legislation and Liberty Vol. 1: Rules and Order*, London 1973, p. 30 (hereafter LLL1).

114. *Errors*, pp. 21–3. See also LLL3, p. 66.

to knowing that, and is based on local tacit knowledge rather than epistemological certainty.[115] Institutions and practices are the decisive determinants of the historical survival of a culture for 'what made men good is neither nature nor reason but tradition'.[116] Only through rules protecting decentralized decision-making can a social order be sustained, diverse cultural resources protected and new knowledge created. Reason is the recognition of the limits of rationality.[117] Rationality refers to the means adopted to fulfil interests and reason refers to the framework of rules within which they can be legitimately enacted. Hayek thus works with a conception of culture which is humanly constructed but not rationally designed.

The theory developed here shares common ground with many of Hayek's assumptions. These include the role of societal traditions in the preservation of knowledge, the critique of the state as a rational planner, the concept of decentralized diversity and the role of individual rights as rules of just association. The difference lies in the opposition that Hayek creates between the state as a rational constructor and the market as a spontaneous order. While in his epistemology he creates a third way between instinct and reason which he calls tradition, in his social theory there is no parallel mediating principle between statism and the market.[118] Vocational organizations, public libraries, universities, artisan institutions and municipal government are denied their status as decentralized organizations which distribute knowledge and preserve traditions. The equation of society and the market is the cause of his conflation of information and knowledge. Information refers to a series of signs and representations, knowledge is the substantive set of practices which assimilates and judges the relevant data. Only through the integration of knowledge-based institutions within the economy can new information be effectively incorporated into the practices of production.[119] In exclusively stressing the

---

115. See Michael Polanyi, *Personal Knowledge*, London 1958.

116. LLL3, p. 160. LLL1, pp. 20–7.

117. Hayek writes that: 'It has always been a recognition of the limits of the possible which has enabled man to make full use of his powers.' LLL1, p. 8. Also LLL3, p. 29.

118. F.A. Hayek, *The Three Sources of Human Values*, London 1978. Also see *Errors*, pp. 21, 73.

119. The elimination of societal institutions from the concept of tradition derives from Hayek's methodological inability to distinguish between the formal and substantive conceptions of the economic developed in pp. 5–19.

procedure through which signals are disseminated, Hayek is incapable of defining the institutional means through which substantive practices of practical knowledge have been protected from the rationality of the market as well as the rationalism of the state. He defines institutions which protect productive practices as interferences with the efficient distribution of information. This leads to Hayek's elimination of practical knowledge from the definition of tradition and the subsequent adoption of an entirely abstract conception of tradition and culture.

Culture, Hayek argues, is 'a tradition of learnt rules of conduct', yet in principle there can be no account of how such education is maintained, for traditions are denied any practical institutional embodiment.[120] Hayek's epistemology thus provides the foundation for the rejection of his social and economic theory. He cannot provide an account of the role of scientific, vocational and municipal institutions which constrain the formation of factor markets in labour and land while enhancing production and knowledge. Neither can he account for the role that state recognition of autonomous institutions can play as an alternative to centralized direction.

The historical argument presented here claims that the growth of knowledge and of new methods of production have been protected, developed and disseminated through non-market institutions which regulate the supply and distribution of skills. Vocational organizations protect the cultural diversity necessary for successful adaptation and preserve the values of honesty, promise-keeping and obedience to learnt rules which Hayek claims are vital for the survival of extended orders of economic co-operation. He argues that it is the lack of virtue within society that is ultimately ruinous for socialism.[121] The ethical collapse arising from the administrative demolition of the self-organized traditions constitutive of society leads 'to the degeneration and destruction of all morals'.[122] It is argued here that the lack of virtue generated by the abolition of the decentralized institutions of society is ruinous for a market order. The ultimate choice facing society, Hayek argues, is between the constructivist rationalism of the state and

---

120. LLL3, p. 33.
121. LLL3, p. 170.
122. LLL3, p. 172.

the spontaneous diversity of the market.[123] The choice presented here is between a virtue and a virtual economy.

Statecraft, vocation and the supply of skill

When looking for causes of sustained productivity success, attention will be given throughout this book to the institutions which promote virtue within the supply side of the economy. It will be argued in chapter three that the national skill formation generated by the training and occupational structure of German economic institutions distinguishes it from its less robust competitors.[124] Ideas of vocation and virtue are retained in the legal code of the state and the internal organization of the enterprise.

It is assumed that state direction of the economy reduces virtue through its reliance on criteria external to the practices of production and a scale of organization inhospitable to the demand for decentralized adaptation generated by the volatility of technology and demand. It is also argued that the state has a vital supply-side role in the recognition of institutions which promote public goods within the economy. One of the conclusions arising from this analysis is that public institutions and political decision have a significant effect on economic outcome.

---

123. LLL3, p. 154.
124. See chapter three.

The Church and Labour

From 1848 to 1948: The Resources of Renewal

The Paris uprising of May 1848 was undertaken in the name of freeing Poland from foreign occupation.[1] The rebels' more local concern was that the proclamations issued the previous February concerning rights of employment and association had been withdrawn by the new government.[2] The 'Democratic and Social' Republic was dissolved, the National Assembly was disbanded, all forms of labour association banned and freedom of speech suspended.[3] The idea of justice advocated by the Catholic and socialist participants in the uprisings of May and June 1848 in France represented an original reconciliation of the conflicting demands of liberty and democracy.[4] They defended the individual rights of

---

1. For an account of the support of the Parisian workers for Polish independence and the affinities of Polish intellectuals with its ideals see Peter Brock, 'The Socialists of the Polish Great Immigration' in Asa Briggs and John Saville, eds, *Essays in Labour History*, London 1967, pp. 140–73.

2. See Roger Magraw, *A History of the French Working-Class. Vol. 2: The Age of the Artisan Radicals*, Oxford 1992, pp. 147–60 (hereafter Magraw).

3. See William H. Sewell Jr., *Work and Revolution in France: The Language of Labour from the Old Regime to 1848*, Cambridge 1981, chapters nine and ten (hereafter Sewell). Magraw, pp. 131–6.

4. Louis Blanc wrote in 1848 that: 'Freedom consists, not only in the rights that have been accorded, but also in the power given men to develop and exercise their faculties, under the reign of justice and the safeguard of law . . . For once it is admitted that a man must have the power to develop and exercise his faculties in order to be really free, the upshot is that society owes every one of its members both instruction, without which the human mind cannot grow, and the instruments of labour, without which human activity cannot achieve its fullest development.' Louis Blanc, 'The Organisation of Labour' in A. Fried and R. Sanders, eds, *Socialist Thought: A Documentary History*, New York 1992, pp. 231–7, p. 235.

expression, worship and association and located democracy in the community of work.[5] It was only after 1848 that the concept of fraternity was tacked onto liberty and equality to complete the revolutionary trilogy.[6]

The ideology of 1848 with its mixture of economic syndicalism, religious toleration and political liberalism was the failure against which all the significant European ideologies measured themselves in the next 150 years, sharing only a consensus on its futility. For Marx it signified a heroic but doomed attempt to recreate the pre-industrial past.[7] Socialism, he argued, was utopian if it held that there was a possibility of continuity between the world of the city and that of citizenship. Liberalism developed towards centralized citizenship and economic atomization.[8] Nationalism concerned itself with the construction of an abstract generalized community embodied in the state.[9] The men who marched outside the Hotel de Ville under the banners of their trade, with Jesus the 'divine proletarian' as their common saint, were the failure against which modern ideologies measured their success.[10] Yet none of the unstable solutions that followed the joint sovereignty of states and markets over society could eradicate the unity of rights and democracy first articulated in 1848.

---

5. Sewell, p. 263.

6. Fraternity re-established the non-contractual ties that the revolution of reason had abolished. It evoked the relations between workers in the outlawed corporations, the solidarity of Christian community that the new state had disavowed and the filial bonds of a traditional political society. See V. Muñoz Dardé, *Fraternité, Un concept politique?*, Paris 1997, chapter one.

7. Marx wrote: 'The bourgeoisie has resolved personal worth into exchange value and in place of the numberless indefeasible chartered freedoms has set up that single unconscionable freedom - Free Trade.' Karl Marx and Friedrich Engels, *Manifesto of the Communist Party*, London 1996, p. 7.

8. See chapter one, pp. 5–19.

9. A good account of the nationalist position is given in Roman Szporluk, *Communism and Nationalism: Karl Marx Versus Friedrich List*, Oxford 1988.

10. For this description of Jesus see Sewell, p. 239. An analysis of the depiction of Christ as a worker is given in F. Berenson, *Populist Religion and Left-Wing Politics in France 1830–52*, New Jersey 1982. The painter Esquinos was jailed for his work 'Evangile du peuple' which portrayed Jesus as a sansculotte in 1841 (Magraw, p. 76). Moss argues that 'federalist trade socialism' remained the fundamental medium of French working-class politics until the First World War. See Bernard H. Moss, *The Origins of the French Labour Movement: The Socialism of Skilled Workers 1830–1914*, Berkeley 1976.

The early labour movement in Britain argued that the King, clergy and flag were not the basis of state power and proposed in contrast the natural rights of man as well as those of 'freeborn Englishmen'.[11] They drew upon values of solidarity and trust that the commodification of society during the enclosure movement and industrialization had appeared to destroy, as well as ideals of political liberalism that were denied recognition as part of the national culture by the robust traditionalism propounded by the monarchy, Church and aristocracy.[12] A communitarian state and an individualistic economy, they argued, denied their needs and freedom.[13] Democracy was located in the economy and liberty in the state.[14] The Chartists, the co-operative movement and the Owenites, all argued for the extension of individual rights and the widening of the suffrage.[15] They also argued for a democratic economy through the idea of city and village-based communities of trade.[16] The radicalism common to Paine, Cobbett, Spence and Thelwall was animated by a desire to reconcile rights and democracy through a resistance to the market as the sole distributor of

---

11. E.P. Thompson claims that Thomas Paine's *The Rights of Man* (1791) was the 'foundation of the English Working-Class Movement'. See T*he Making of the English Working Class*, New York 1963, p. 90. The hold of Natural Law is brought out in the petition drawn up by the London Workingmen's Association in 1837 which was the basis of the charter presented to Parliament: 'The universal political right of every human being is superior and stands apart from all customs, forms or ancient usage, a fundamental right not in the power of man to confer; or justly to deprive him of. That to take away this sacred right from the person and to vest it in *property*, is a wilful perversion of justice and common sense, as the creation and security of property *are the consequences of society*.' In *Socialist Thought*, pp. 187–8. Emphasis in the original.

12. See John Saville, *1848: The British State and the Chartist Movement*, Cambridge 1987.

13. See T. Spence, 'The Real Rights of Man', in *The Political Work of Thomas Spence*, ed. H.T. Dickinson, Newcastle Upon Tyne 1982.

14. See Noel Thompson, *The People's Science: The Popular Political Economy of Exploitation and Crisis 1816-1834*, Cambridge 1984, chapter four.

15. See D. Goodway, *London Chartism 1838–1848*, Cambridge 1982. See also G.D.H. Cole, *The History of Socialist Thought, Vol. 1: The Forerunners, 1789–1850*, London 1953.

16. See Malcom Chase, *'The People's Farm': English Radical Agrarianism 1775–1840*, Oxford 1988. See also the article by E.P. Thompson, 'The Moral Economy of the English Crowd in the Eighteenth Century', *Past and Present*, No. 50, 1971.

material goods in society and the state as the ultimate source of communal identity.[17]

In Germany in 1948, the ideas of democratic vocational self-government and individual rights first expressed in 1848 became the institutional and ethical means of reconstructing society.[18] Through this tradition society could be restored without resorting to communitarian nationalism or market atomization. The common ground between socialists and Catholics in Germany was that both traditions had resisted state centralization and market competition since 1848 by making the vocation (*Beruf*) their central unit of economic association.[19] They were consistently defeated, yet in 1945 it was the Catholic Church and the trade unions who provided the social theory and ethical practices that characterized the distinctive economic and welfare institutions constitutive of West Germany after the defeat of Nazism. These two traditions formed the identity of the country's two main political parties and provided the moral and intellectual ideals and organizations that underpinned what became known as the social-market economy.[20] At the centenary of its defeat, a fragmented nation turned to the principles of 1848 for their resources of renewal.[21]

---

17. See Gregory Claeys, *Machinery, Money and the Millennium: From Moral Economy to Socialism*, Cambridge 1987, pp. 184–95. See also Iain Hampshire Monk, 'John Thelwall and the Eighteenth Century Response to Political Economy', *Historical Journal*, Vol. 45, 1991, pp. 1–20.

18. See this chapter, pp. 43–50. Also see chapter three, pp. 64–82.

19. See Ralph H. Bowen, *German Theories of the Corporate State: With Special Reference to the Period 1870–1914*, New York 1947 (hereafter Bowen), pp. 53–8. Also Rudolph Stadelmann, *Social and Political History of the German 1848 Revolution*, trans. James Chastain, Ohio 1975, pp 159–7.

20. The concept of the social-market economy was first coined by Alfred Müller-Armack in 1947. He wrote: 'We need a novel synthesis of security and freedom which will make it possible for us to combine more socialism with more freedom. This is, however, only possible on the basis of a socially guided market economy.' Quoted in Rudolph Walther, 'Economic Liberalism', *Economy and Society*, Vol. 13, No. 2, 1984, p. 205. See also A.J. Nicholls, *Freedom with Responsibility: The Social Market in Germany 1918–1963*, Oxford 1994 (hereafter Nicholls) pp. 120–1. Keith Tribe, 'The Genealogy of the Social Market Economy: 1937–48', in *Strategies of Economic Order: German Economic Discourse 1750–1950*, Cambridge 1995, pp. 203–40, p. 204. It is argued in pp. 50–55 that this idea was far from mainstream liberalism and was subordinate to longer-standing traditions and practices in the reconstruction of West German society.

21. See chapter three.

Social and Christian Democrats defined the dominant problem of modern society as a reconciliation of the market with a form of solidarity which did not descend into state authoritarianism. The solution proposed, that of political liberalism and social democracy, does not indicate agreement on how to define the 'social' or the organizations which best preserve solidarity. The institutional role of the Church was disputed between them, as was the status of agriculture and the organization of education and welfare.[22] Socialism and Christian social teaching were united, however, in their intention to preserve what economic liberals denied existed: a society with organized patterns of knowledge which functioned outside the sovereignty of the market yet could resist domination by the state. They pointed to the immorality as well as the unviability of a society based on a statist conception of community and an individualist conception of economic dynamism. The recognition of self-organized apprenticeship and insurance systems, co-determination in industry and strong city and regional government became defining features of the social-market economy and were created by the ideological congruence of social Catholicism and social democracy.

The two cultural traditions that shaped the economic organization of the Federal Republic had played a beleaguered role in Germany since unification in 1871. Both the Catholic Church and the labour movement had been defined as alien to the national identity. The anti-socialist Exclusion Laws of 1878 and the Protestant ascendancy enforced through the *Kulturkampf* were central features of the new polity. In the words of Blackbourn:

> The 1880s saw successive onslaughts against Catholics and the Labour Movement in which major parts of the newly unified population were treated not so much as dissident citizens, but effectively as inhabitants of an occupied state.[23]

The experience of finding themselves at home in an alien nation led to the development of sophisticated social theories and dense

---

22. See A. Hussain and K. Tribe, *Marxism and the Agrarian Question*, London 1983. Hussain argues that Social Democracy supported the small peasantry in the eastern lands against the large owners, pp. 133–8.

23. David Blackbourn, *Class, Religion and Local Politics in Wilhelmine Germany: The Centre Party in Württemberg before 1914*, New Jersey 1989, p. 9.

networks of vocational and confessional association which disputed the sovereignty of the nation-state.[24] Their opposition was based on ideals of international and local solidarity, a historical conception of state authority and the idea that organizations in society had an ethical status.[25] The Church and Labour also represented the poorest parts of the population (Catholic peasants and workers of all faiths) whose status was made considerably more insecure by the formation of a national market. Given their minority status, socialist and Catholic movements were compelled to lead efforts for the establishment of the civil rights of association and worship as well as the demands for welfare guarantees against destitution and unemployment.[26]

Christian Democracy: Solidarity, Subsidiarity and Status

The first tradition out of which the institutions of the social-market economy were fashioned was that of Christian Democracy. It will be argued in this section that Christian Democracy was already a distinctive ideology at the time of the Paris uprising in 1848.[27] Its distinction was based on developing an initially dissident interpretation of Catholic teaching which opposed the indissoluble tie to the monarchy and sought to incorporate labour organizations within its structure. Its philosophical and sociological analysis meant that it was capable of explaining and participating in the process of industrialization by making what it defined as the 'social' question, or more specifically the 'labour' question, its central concern. Its doctrine may be summarized as

---

24. For a review of new work on Catholic associationism see Eric Yonke, 'The Catholic Sub-Culture in Modern Germany: Recent Work in the Social History of Religion', *Catholic Historical Review*, Vol. 80, No. 3, 1994, pp. 534–45. Also see Margaret Anderson, 'Piety and Politics: Recent Work on German Catholicism', *Journal of Modern History*, Vol. 63, 1991, pp. 681–786.

25. For the anti-statist component in both socialist and Catholic thought see Bowen, p. 216.

26. For an account of the relationship between the Catholic Church and the development of social policy see Franz-Xaver Kaufmann, 'The Churches and the Emergent Welfare State in Germany' *ISB Materialien No. 11*, Institut für Bevölkerungsforschung und Sozialpolitik, Bielefeld 1983.

27. See Hans Maier, *Revolution and Church: The Early History of Christian Democracy, 1789–1901*, Notre Dame 1969, pp. 68–140, 290–8 (hereafter Maier).

the subordination of both state and market to a self-governing society through the cultivation of solidarity.

The argument proposed by Christian Democracy was that private property could only be preserved if the rights of capital were constrained.[28] It was an ideology founded upon the resistance to 'proletarianization', defined as the unmediated dependence on a wage for survival.[29] Drawing upon the idea that the person is a social rather than a political being, they argued that ethics were best preserved within the organizations of society. The ideology that had been condemned in 1834 by Pope Gregory XVI as 'false, calumnious, rash, anarchic, contrary to the word of God, impious, scandalous and erroneous' had become mainstream Church teaching by 1944.[30] While in its political philosophy it added little to Locke's definition of natural law, its social theory was more original.[31]

Paris 1848

The term Christian Democracy (*Démocratie Chrétienne*) was first used to designate a unified political philosophy and social movement during the Paris uprising of 1848.[32] It drew upon the works of Lamennais and his moral affirmation of democracy as based on Christian teaching.[33] The role of democracy, as a

28. The definitive encyclical was Pope Leo XIII, *Rerum Novarum: The Condition of Labour*, (1891) in David J. O'Brien and Thomas A. Shannon, eds, *Catholic Social Thought*, New York 1992, pp. 14–40, p. 21.

29. For the argument that deproletarianization was the central feature of Christian Democracy see Richard Camp, *The Papal Ideology of Social Reform: A Study in Historical Development*, Leiden 1969. See also Donal Dorr, *Options for the Poor: A Hundred Years of Vatican Social Teaching*, Dublin 1983.

30. Pius XII declared in 1944 that democratic participation in the economy was a proper means for carrying out 'just social reforms' and that the liberal-democratic state 'is considered by many to be a natural postulate of reason itself'. See also Kees Van Kersbergen, *Social Capitalism: A Study of Christian Democracy and the Welfare State*, London 1996, p. 93, f.9, p. 87 (hereafter Kersbergen). Bowen, p. 3.

31. For the connection between Catholic and Lockean thought see A.M.C. Waterman, 'John Locke's Theory of Property and Christian Social Thought', *Review of Social Economy*, Vol. 40, 1982, pp. 97–115.

32. See J.B. Duroselle, *Les débuts du Catholique Social en France (1822–1870)*, Paris 1951.

33. Maier, p. 188. F.R. de Lamennais founded the journal *Avenir* which developed the ideology of political decentralization, communal self-administration, individual rights and the importance of intermediate communities between the individual and the state. This became known as 'associationism'. See Magraw, pp. 73–8.

procedure of negotiation between conflicting organizations and interests in society, became one of its distinctive features, the affirmation of civil rights the other. The reconciliation with Republicanism by Catholic activists was not unconditional. The Revolution of 1789, they argued, had a moral quality as an institutional fulfilment of freedom and equality, both of which were based on Gospel teaching.[34] The Revolution, however, was unfinished, for it allowed a social inequality incompatible with citizenship. The old networks of Church, vocational and elite charity had broken down without an effective system of poor relief emerging to replace it.[35] The principle of fraternity, they argued, provided the link between liberty and equality in the form of vocational, professional and welfare associations.[36] This offered the possibility of the Church, which was an extended form of plural voluntary association based upon the concept of fraternity, to renew its pastoral mission to the poor in defending the associations of family and trade unions while upholding the political priority of right.

The following five assumptions distinguished Christian Democracy by 1848. The first was the primacy of society to the state. The second was the complementarity of human rights and civic duties. The third was a rejection of Republican Virtue and the affirmation of the limits of state sovereignty by upholding rights of association, worship and expression. The fourth commitment was to decentralized associations that mediated between the individual and the state, an idea that was initially expressed through the idea of fraternity and later developed into the ideas of solidarity and subsidiarity. The fifth idea was that the conflict between capital and labour could be mediated through the democratic organization of work and the preservation of the status of the worker in defiance of proletarianization. The term *proletaire*, referring to the lowest class of Roman citizens whose only duty was to offer their children to the state, was first used in its modern form by Lamennais in the 1820s to describe the condition of labour in the early-nineteenth-century towns.[37] Christian Democracy was

---

34. Magraw, p. 75.
35. See A. Forest, *The French Revolution and the Poor*, London 1981, chapters one and three.
36. Magraw, pp. 140–1.
37. See G. Briefs, *The Proletariat*, New York 1937, p. 12.

distinguished by the method of balancing conflict within society through democratizing the relationship between employers and labour.[38]

The development of Christian Democracy in Germany

The Catholic critique of capitalism was developed in Germany by Bishop Wilhelm Emmanuel von Ketteler of Mainz.[39] Ketteler defined the 'proletarian' problem as the central concern of Catholic social teaching and argued that in the absence of the welfare previously provided by local communities through charity, people would become directly dependent on the owners of capital for survival.[40] The dilemma of Christian Democracy was that the principle of private property had led to the removal of people's status as members of organizations. A contract between someone who owns the means of subsistence and someone who is compelled to sell their labour through a lack of alternative reserves is not voluntary and exerts its compulsion, not by rational agreement to common rules as is the case of political justice, but through the manipulation of needs within the economy.[41] Due to the scale of modern society, Ketteler argued, the needs of the poor could no longer be met by charity alone.[42]

Unnecessary suffering, Ketteler argued, prevails when the individual is denied justice and the possibility of participating in society as a person capable of trust, conscience and skill. If workers were denied the status of partners in society then they were excluded from the associative activity through which they achieved the status of a person.[43] Work was defined as the activity through

---

38. See P.E. Sigmund, 'The Catholic Tradition and Modern Democracy', *Review of Politics*, Vol. 49, No. 4, 1987, pp. 530–48.

39. See William Edward Hogan, *The Development of Bishop Wilhelm Emmanuel Von Ketteler's Interpretation of the Social Problem*, Washington DC 1946, p. 86 (hereafter Hogan).

40. Wilhelm Emmanuel von Ketteler, *Die Arbeitfrage und Das Christenthum*, Mainz 1864, pp. 49–50.

41. This was developed by Pope Leo XIII in *Rerum Novarum*, p. 26. For the influence of Ketteler on Leo XIII see Hogan, pp. 236–54.

42. Ketteler, *Die Arbeitfrage*, pp. 111–17.

43. Ketteler pointed to the slavery of antiquity as a warning to those who defended the supreme moral value of citizenship. Athens and Rome were characterized by the overriding importance of the *Polis*, a lack of ability to distinguish

which people overcome the dominion of nature by establishing patterns of mutual dependency. Labour was thus an attribute that defined the person.

Labour is the man himself, an essential part of his personality. In a civilized land, therefore, labour must be protected by law. Where this does not obtain, where labour is considered a mere commodity and the capitalist can exploit the worker and slowly destroy his ability to work, there exists in that land, despite all its allegations of civilization, a good beginning toward the most despicable barbarism.[44]

Ketteler thus considered work as an 'essential part' of having a personality. It was a calling accorded dignity as a means of realizing human capabilities. The role of trade unions or artisan associations was to ensure high quality of craftsmanship, honesty in relation to other workers and the preservation of values within the economy.

The important theological work undertaken by Ketteler was the link he established between the Catholic theory of the person and the institutional arrangements required for facilitating the reciprocal development of personality and association.[45] The person, defined as a subjective, rational, purposive agent, could only realize their potential through active association with others. The preservation of vocational institutions which protected the status of the worker was based on the 'principle of association', which Ketteler claimed was the 'natural law of humanity'.[46] He recognized that the consequence of upholding private property had been the removal of other rights, particularly concerning status and subsistence. In as much as the market violated the capacity of the person to live an autonomous life, it was just to rectify this. Ketteler wrote in 1867 that: 'The state through its legislation rendered the worker without appeal before the law; the state is, therefore, under obligation to contribute to the re-establishment of the rights of the labourer before the law.'[47] The obligation was

---

between man and citizen and disrespect for work and workers. He argued that Christianity was the principle force in the dissolution of slavery past and present. Modern liberalism combined the worst of both worlds, pagan state worship with economic barbarism. See *Die Arbeitfrage*, pp. 107–8, 149–56.

44. Quoted in Hogan, p. 155.
45. Ketteler, *Die Arbeitfrage*, pp. 121–37.
46. Ketteler, *Die Arbeitfrage*, p. 16.
47. Quoted in Hogan, p. 155. See also Bowen, p. 79.

all the greater as those who had lost the rights were also the poorest. This idea became central to Catholic social teaching and provided the organizing principle for the subsequent papal encyclicals *Rerum Novarum: The Condition of Labour* (1891), *Quadragesimo Anno: On the Fortieth Anniversary of Rerum Novarum* (1931), *Centesimis Annus: On the Hundredth Anniversary of Rerum Novarum* (1991) and *Laborem Exercens: On Human Work* (1981).[48] In this Pope John-Paul II writes:

> Man is a person, that is to say a subjective being capable of acting in a planned and rational way, capable of deciding about himself and with a tendency to self-realization. As a person man is the subject of work . . . these acts serve to realise his humanity, to fulfil a calling to be a person that is his by reason of his very humanity.[49]

The associations necessary for the development of personality are plurally conceived. Territorially they range from the locality through the municipality, city, region, state and ultimately international institutions.[50] It is on the basis of the idea of the person as an autonomous social being that the priority of labour to capital is asserted by Catholic social teaching. This idea was recently reaffirmed by John-Paul II who wrote that: 'Labour is a primary efficient cause, while capital, the whole collection of means of production, remains a mere instrument or instrumental cause.'[51]

The argument developed by Leo XIII in *Rerum Novarum* was that a reconciliation between rich and poor could only be effected in a market economy through the reciprocal recognition of institutions which represent the interests of classes.[52] The establishment of trade-union representation within the management of the economy and the firm was the institutional means of preserving societal solidarity through overcoming the antagonism between those who

---

48. These are collected in O'Brien and Shannon, eds, *Catholic Social Thought*.

49. John-Paul II, *Laborem Exercens: On Human Work*, (1981) in O'Brien and Shannon, eds, *Catholic Social Thought*, pp. 352–92, p. 358. See also John-Paul II, *Centesimis Annus: On the Hundredth Anniversary of Rerum Novarum* (1991) in O'Brien and Shannon, *Catholic Social Thought*, pp. 439–88.

50. Christian Democrats have been in the vanguard of European integration, which is consistent with their instrumental attitude to the state.

51. John-Paul II, *Laborem Exercens*, p. 362.

52. Leo XIII, *Rerum Novarum*, p. 21. Ketteler, *Die Arbeitfrage*, pp. 85–6.

owned and those compelled to labour for survival.[53] Ketteler and Leo XIII, both working within Thomist premises, argued that there was a distinction between ownership and use rights.[54] A distinction was made between private property and capital, between that which provided a daily sphere of autonomy such as a home and possessions, and that which organized the relationship between groups in society, such as the ownership of the means of subsistence or technology. Ketteler defended private property through resisting the rights of capital. The solution to societal dissolution was the preservation of status within publicly recognized associations with a function in the economy.

On this basis Ketteler could develop a distinctive position that shared with socialists a critique of capitalism but which could also oppose statist welfare solutions by redefining the Church's role in society as a distributor of welfare. The right to life meant that the claim to subsistence was a matter of justice not of altruism. The distribution of welfare did not necessarily have to be administered by the state, although it was dependent upon its financial support. The subsidiarity principle justified a subsidy to societal institutions and by means of transfer payments they could administer the welfare rights through an expansion of the role of self-organized institutions. Ketteler actively sought the construction of Christian labour unions which became a significant force within the Centre (*Zentrum*) Party during the Weimar period. Catholic associations were particularly strong in the *Handwerk*, metalwork and agricultural sectors.[55]

---

53. These ideas are developed in J. Boswell, *Community and the Economy: The Theory of Public Co-operation*, London 1990. See also P. Milner, *Social Catholicism in Europe*, London 1991.

54. Aquinas argued that if a person is in need, 'he may take what is necessary from another person's goods, either openly or by stealth. Nor is this, strictly speaking, fraud or robbery.' *Aquinas*, ed. A.P. D'Entreves, Oxford 1978, p. 171. Aquinas follows Aristotle in arguing that exchange for the satisfaction of needs is legitimate and exchange exclusively for profit is potentially corrupting.

55. See Michael Schneider, *Die Christlichen Gewerkschaften 1894–1933*, Bonn 1982, pp. 768–71. For an account of the strengths and weaknesses of the Catholic labour movement after 1914 see William L. Patch, *Christian Trade Unions in the Weimar Republic 1918–1933: The Failure of 'Corporate Pluralism'*, New Haven 1985.

Christian Democracy

After 1945, the newly established Christian Democratic Union (*Christlich-Demokratische Union*) stressed the value of solidarity, which was to be sustained by subsidiarity and organized through the preservation of status. The anonymous distribution of misfortune resulting from the creation of unplanned markets, it was argued, could be generalized in the provision of guarantees against calamity in the form of welfare.[56] This was justified by defending the proposition that society is characterized by a dependence on others for survival and that this demanded a shared responsibility for their fate.[57] The Christian Democratic conception of solidarity stresses the constraints on freedom resulting from dependency and the institutions necessary to prevent the necessity of association from becoming a form of domination. A person without institutional protection in the form of legal and democratic rights had no power in negotiating fair terms of social co-operation. Solidarity was thus institutionalized through the generalization of risk in the form of welfare guarantees justified by a conscious sharing of the hazards and burdens of collective association. This was achieved through the distribution of rights to all citizens as members of a state and the sharing of material burdens as members of society. The demand of justice was to provide the material preconditions for effective participation in society as well as an equal status before the law.

The subsidiarity principle (*Subsidiaritätsprinzip*) is the idea that power should be decentralized and decisions made at the most immediate level possible and only become further removed if they are impossible to fulfil.[58] This was institutionalized through regional federalism, the vocational organization of insurance and the democratic organization of the enterprise. The role of the state was to subsidize the smaller organizations of society and cultivate

---

56. See chapter three, pp. 79–82.

57. For the idea of 'social insurance' and the generalization of risk as expressed in pension schemes see Jacques Donzelot, 'The Promotion of the Social', *Economy and Society*, Vol. 17, No. 3, 1988, pp. 395–427.

58. For an analysis of subsidiarity see Guido Dierickx, 'Christian Democracy and Its Ideological Rivals', in David Hanley, ed., *Christian Democracy in Europe: A Comparative Perspective*, London 1994, pp. 15–30. Also see Kees van Kersbergen, 'The Distinctiveness of Christian Democracy', ibid., pp 31–50.

decentralization through sustaining existing groups. Large authorities supplement smaller ones rather than incorporate or direct them. Transfer payments replace direct state administration as the obligation of justice does not specify the instrument of administration. Christian Democracy defined the responsibility of the state as the preservation of the decentralized democratic institutions that distribute skills, knowledge and material goods. Subsidized subsidiarity renews the threatened institutions which underpin societal solidarity.[59] Christian Democrats thus opposed unmediated dependence on the state by developing institutions which could resist market sovereignty.

Status was preserved in the industrial sector through partnership in the democratic organization of industry in terms of collective bargaining, representation on the boards of management, factory-level works councils and the democratic administration of pension funds. It was further expressed through the protection of artisans by means of the enforcement of licensed apprenticeships as a condition of market participation, as well as the idea of citizenship as a generalized status demanding rights and duties.[60] Subsidiarity, the preservation of vocational status and the defence of individual rights became an important aspect of Christian Democratic ideology by 1948. No force within the Church successfully challenged Christian Democracy as its political representative. It fostered a set of practices, institutions and values that served as strong cultural determinants of the political and economic organizational forms of the Federal Republic.

Adenauer's subsequent influence on the Christian Democratic Union (CDU) should not obscure the initial strength of the radical Catholic wing of the party, particularly in the British sector which became North Rhine Westphalia.[61] The Walberberg circle of Dominican resistance fighters founded the first post-war Christian Democratic Party.[62] Their 'Christian socialism' was based on a programme of industrial self-government by labour

---

59. See Maier, p. 37.
60. See section on Handwerk in the next chapter.
61. When Adenauer was asked in the immediate post-war years which British political party he felt the CDU were closest to he replied 'Labour'. In H.C. Wolf, 'The Lucky Miracle: Germany 1945–1951' in R. Dornbusch, W. Nölling and R. Layard, eds, *Post-war Reconstruction and Lessons for the East Today*, Cambridge Mass. 1993, pp. 29–56, p 52 f. 13 (hereafter Wolf).
62. See Kersbergen, p. 43.

and capital.[63] They remained the dominant Christian Democratic force in North Rhine Westphalia until 1949 and formed an important part of the Christian Democratic Union that wrote the Ahlen programme in 1946.[64] Karl Arnold, a leader of the Catholic trade union before 1933, was a founder member of the Christian Democratic Party and the prime minister of North Rhine Westphalia from 1947. His proposal for the establishment of democratic parity control in all the economic institutions within the *Land* was vetoed by the British in 1949.[65] The CDU/CSU (Bavarian Christian Social Union) programme of 1949 called for the socialization of natural resources, co-determination of industry and the public control of monopoly industries.

Social Democracy: Works Councils, Citizenship and the Labour Movement

The theory of justice advanced by the artisan masters and journeymen at their Congress in Frankfurt in 1848 combined political liberalism with vocational democracy.[66] They called for a progressive income and property tax, the establishment of free education, a common system of weights and measures, a national currency and the promotion of employment by the state in the form of public works programmes. They also called for the establishment of compensation for those who were incapacitated by illness or accidents. A proposal was submitted to the National Assembly which approved of the compulsory issue of work rules by a factory committee consisting of owners and elected representatives of the employees and the restoration of artisan licensing rights.[67]

---

63. See Bernd Uhl, *Die Idee des Christlichen Sozialismus in Deutschland, 1945–1947*, Mainz 1975, pp. 17–20.

64. See Kersbergen, p. 229.

65. See Diethelm Prowe, 'Economic Democracy in Post-World War II Germany: Corporatist Crisis Response 1945–48', *Journal of Modern History*, Vol. 57, 1985, pp. 451–82.

66. For a summary of the demands of 1848 see P. H. Noyes, *Organisation and Revolution: Working-Class Associations in the German Revolution of 1848-1849*, Princeton 1966, chapter seven. Also see Barrington Moore Jr, *Injustice: The Social Bases of Obedience and Revolt*, Cambridge 1978, pp. 269–74 (hereafter *Injustice*).

67. See Wolfram Fischer, *Handwerksrecht und Handwerkswirtschaft um 1800: Studien zur Sozial- und Wirtschaftsverfassung vor der industriellen Revolution*, Berlin 1955.

The artisans were committed to a conception of citizenship that remained embedded in the city. The imposition of common rules and rights of work practice were enforced within each city by the chambers (*Kammern*).[68] Their authority was based on two rules. No guild member could trespass on the domain of another and only artisans licensed by the chamber could exercise, within the town, any economic function that belonged to the guild. The masters conceded that there was legitimate competition, which took place between appropriately qualified citizens thus protecting the public against fraud, cheating and shoddy workmanship. Through their sanctions of expulsion and their responsibility for apprenticeship, chambers enjoyed considerable authority in the organization of economic production and the distribution of welfare.[69] A Republican conception of citizenship was combined with an embedded notion of economic organization. The persistence of craft unions and craft production remained a significant aspect of German economic production and framed the development of industrial trade unionism.[70]

Although the ideology of the Free Trade Unions (*Allgemeiner Deutscher Gewerkschaftsbund* – ADGB) was Marxist, at no point did it relinquish its 'pre-modern' aspirations to the recognition of skilled status and active participation in the organization of industrial production.[71] The case of the mining industry is illustrative. Resistance to arbitrary managerial methods, far more than wage claims, formed the basis of the major coal strikes on the Ruhr between 1895 and 1920.[72] Central to each was the demand for the

---

68. See chapter three. See also Colin Crouch, 'Co-operation and Competition in an Institutionalised Economy: The Case of Germany', in C. Crouch and D. Marquand, eds, *Ethics and Markets: Co-operation and Competition Within Capitalist Economies*, Oxford 1993, pp. 80–98, p. 86.

69. Mack Walker, *German Home Towns: Community, State and General Estate 1648–1871*, Ithaca 1971.

70. In 1863, there were more craft workers in Lassalle's socialist union than factory workers. Hogan, p. 84.

71. Guillebaud, in his work on the Weimar works council legislation, writes that the declaration of the National Assembly in 1848 calling for worker participation in the management of firms and the recognition of crafts organizations as the principle judges of quality remained 'one of the most keenly desired reforms of the German labour movement'. C.W. Guillebaud, *The Works Councils: A German Experiment in Industrial Democracy*, Cambridge 1928, p. 1 (hereafter Guillebaud).

72. Barrington Moore, *Injustice*, pp. 243–315.

establishment of works councils to help organize the management of the firm.

Between 1776 and 1851 the legal authority of Prussian officials within the mining industry was unconstrained. Outside the workplace miners were granted corporate privileges, army exemption, tax relief and autonomous welfare associations.[73] After 1851 there was a transfer of managerial authority from the state to the private owners, who responded by withdrawing corporate privileges while intensifying managerial prerogative.[74] The 1889 strike resisted the imposition of these new rules.[75] Having initially enforced the imposition of the market, the state began to intervene to protect the workers' status. A mining law was passed in 1892 which stipulated that new working rules could not be introduced without consultation with older workers and granted a 15 per cent increase in pay, an abolition of overtime and the restoration of the eighthour day.[76]

Ultimately the unions did not have the resources to win strikes; they were invariably starved back to work after a month. Their victories lay in concessions won from the state in the regulation of their working conditions once the strike had been defeated. The miners strike of 1905 was over the managerial violation of the 1892 Law. The strike demands were for the democratic election of inspectors and mine supervisors, the creation of workers' committees in each firm to settle disagreements, the dismissal of officials who abused workers and the delivery of coal at cost to the homes of each miner.[77] This was rejected on the basis of management's right to manage. The miners were again defeated within a

---

73. For a description of the miners' welfare organization see J. Tampke, 'Bismarck's Social Legislation: A Genuine Breakthrough?', in W.J. Mommsen, ed., *The Emergence of the Welfare State in Britain and Germany, 1850–1950*, London 1981, pp. 71–83.

74. See M.F. Parnell, *The German Tradition of Organised Capitalism: Self Government in the Coal Industry*, Oxford 1994, p. 15 (hereafter Parnell).

75. See Karl Ditt and Dagmar Kift, eds, *1889: Bergarbeiterstreik und Wilhelminische Gesellschaft*, Hagan 1989.

76. See Albin Gladen, 'Die Streiks der Bergarbeiter im Ruhrgebiet in den Jahren 1889, 1905 und 1912', in J. Rulecke, ed., *Arbeiterbewegung an Rhein und Ruhr: Beiträge zur Geschichte der Arbeiterbewegung in Rheinland-Westfalen*, Wuppertal 1974, pp. 111–48.

77. See M.J. Koch, *Die Bergarbeiterbewegung im Ruhrgebiet zur Zeit Wilhelms II, 1889–1914*, Düsseldorf 1954, pp. 90–1.

month but the government passed a law establishing works committees within each firm and instituted the election of the safety inspectors by the works councils. The sovereignty of the market was curtailed by the will of the state.

The trade unions' political conception of rights and welfare was combined with an economic conception of democratic control of the work environment. The increasingly democratic conception of political citizenship and an ever more administrative notion of economic organization characteristic of the development of Social Democratic ideology conflicted with the authority of the works councils.[78] It was this tension that laid the basis of the conflict between sections of the trade unions and the Social Democratic Party (SPD) government after 1918.[79]

With the defeat of the Imperial Army in 1918 a Republic was proclaimed in Berlin on 9 November. In the absence of any other legitimate and organized political force the SPD inherited the German nation-state. They did not seize power (it was legally handed over to the Social Democrat leader Friedrich Ebert by the Kaiser) and their legitimacy was based on two sources. The first was the National Assembly in Berlin, the second was the workers' and soldiers' councils that were formed within the factories and the ranks of returning troops.[80]

Due to the peculiarities of the situation in 1918, the internal conflicts of the labour movement were fought on the national stage. The point at issue was the status of the works councils (*Betriebsräte*). In 1919 there was a wave of strikes in the coal, metal and chemical industries; the common demand in each was the removal of military forms of management within the firm.[81]

---

78. See H. Tudor and J.M. Tudor, *Marxism and Social-Democracy: The Revisionist Debate*, Cambridge 1988.

79. See W.J. Mommsen, 'The German Revolution 1918–1920: Political Revolution or Social Protest Movement', in R. Bessel and E.J. Feuchtwanger, eds, *Social Change and Political Development in Weimar Germany*, London 1991, pp. 21–34.

80. There was a tremendous growth in trade union membership after 1918. By March 1919 it was twice that of the pre-war total. For an analysis of the conditions of demobilization see Richard Bessel, 'Unemployment and Demobilisation in Germany after the First World War', in R.J. Evans and Dick Geary, eds, *The German Unemployed: Experiences and Consequences of Mass Unemployment from the Weimar Republic to the Third Reich*, London 1987, pp. 23–43.

81. See Jürgen Tampke, *The Ruhr and Revolution: The Revolutionary Movement in the Rhenish Westphalia Industrial Region 1912–1919*, London 1979.

The demand for 'decent human treatment' (*anständige Behandlung*) took the form of the democratization of the firms' command structure concerning safety at work, the setting of piece rates, access to the firms' financial records and a negotiated wage.[82] This was complemented by a common declaration of duties to the efficiency of the firm and its well-being.[83] There was a general strike in support of these goals which was militarily suppressed by the SPD government and the reactivated *Freikorps* in November 1919.[84] Having inherited the nation, the SPD had weakened their links with important sections of its previous support and lost the national election. Their rehabilitation was based on renewing the traditions and institutions they had undermined in the two years after the First World War. The analysis developed by the trade unions was that the Weimar Republic had initially seen substantial improvements in the status of labour within German society.

In November 1918 the organized trade-union movement was recognized for the first time as a legal organization and a negotiating partner by the employers' association.[85] The Central Works Community (ZAG) was continued after the war and given responsibility for demobilization measures. This was a tripartite body made up of employers, unions and the state, through which organized labour participated in the administration of the Republic.[86] The eight-hour day was established. The 1920 Works Council Act was passed which called for the election of works councils in companies with more than twenty employees. A supplementary Act was passed in 1921 stipulating rights of access to balance sheets and profit and loss accounts, and a further Act was passed in 1922 which called for two works councillors to be present on the supervisory boards of companies. The aspiration to the democratic self-administration of industry was outlined in Article 165 of the Weimar Constitution. This stated that the worker 'endeavours to reach out beyond the status of employee and attain a co-operative status in the production process itself'.[87] Under the terms of

---

82. See Peter von Oertzen, *Betriebsräte in der Novemberrevolution*, Düsseldorf 1963, pp. 139–40.
83. See Barrington Moore, *Injustice*, p. 325.
84. Barrington Moore, *Injustice*, pp. 344–53.
85. This was recognized in the Stinnes-Legien Agreement of 1918.
86. See R. Bessel, *Germany After the First World War*, Oxford 1993, pp. 122–38.
87. Guillebaud, p. 11.

the Act, however, works councils had no right to issue orders, interfere with the 'executive function of management' or require the employer to follow its advice in regard to the conduct and organization of the enterprise.[88]

The analysis of the failure of Weimar proposed by the trade unions was that the Labour Law Code was not implemented.[89] The eight-hour day was discarded in 1923 when hours began to rise.[90] The declining power of labour within the industrial cartels following the rise in unemployment in the 1920s led to the further dismantling of welfare guarantees which accelerated under Brüning's and Papen's administrations.[91] The effective opposition of employers to worker participation was undermined by the creation of 'special' management committees which were established in order to 'circumvent clear statutory provisions'.[92] As Dartmann puts it:

> Because of its limited enforceability and widespread employer evasion of the more important provisions of the Acts, mainly through the transfer of important decisions from the supervisory boards to committees to which no works councils were admitted, the experiment of works councils was regarded by the official trade union movement either negatively or as an issue of lesser value and interest.[93]

For these reasons the experiment in co-operation was seen as inadequate, the conclusion being that worker representation had to be extended and strengthened.[94]

---

88. Guillebaud, p. 21. Also, Parnell, p. 58.

89. See Ludwig Preller, *Sozialpolitik in der Weimarer Republik*, Stuttgart 1949, p. 245.

90. Christoph Dartmann, 'Redistribution of Power, Joint Consultation or Productivity Coalition? Labour and Post-War reconstruction in Germany and Britain, 1945–1953', Bochum 1996 (hereafter Dartmann), p. 32. See Hans Mommsen, 'Class War or Co-determination: On the Control of Economic Power in the Weimar Republic', in Mommsen, *From Weimar to Auschwitz*, Cambridge 1992, pp. 62–78, p. 74.

91. See Mommsen, 'Class War or Co-determination', pp. 70–7.

92. Mommsen, 'Class War or Co-determination', p. 72.

93. Dartmann, p. 26.

94. Guillebaud wrote of the 1919 Works Council Act that it: 'appeared to most of its supporters as but an anaemic and sickly child, quite unworthy of the parent ideas as expressed in Article 165 of the Constitution and the revolutionary spirit which helped to inspire that article'. Guillebaud, p. 13.

The interpretation of the defects of the Weimar Republic developed in Germany by the labour movement are of fundamental importance in explaining the development of the Federal Republic after 1945. The inadequacies were perceived at the time. Fritz Naphtali, the head of the policy section of the ADGB, developed the idea of economic democracy (*Wirtschaftsdemokratie*) which was adopted in 1925.[95] This sought to reconcile the role of the state and the decentralization of power required by workplace authority.[96] By stressing its potential for increasing efficiency, modernizing skills and developing industry the SPD was pacified. By providing greater control over working life through the establishment of factory councils, the trade-union demand for control of the work environment was satisfied.[97] In this way democratic industrial organization was restored as a feature of Social Democratic policy and a more harmonious relationship developed between party and movement. This was adopted as union policy before the successes of Nazism precluded the practical prospect of its implementation.

The explanation of the rise of Fascism proposed by the trade unions was founded upon the assumption that the state and the owners of industry joined forces against the democratic labour movement.[98] The unions thought it foolish to allow this alliance to be formed once more. The joint management of industry by unions and employers was the preferred solution as it both excluded the state from direct interference and fixed the employers as an equal partner dependent upon union support. This institutionalized the power of trade unions in the economy

---

95. Fritz Naphtali, *Wirtschaftsdemokratie, Ihr Wesen, Weg und Ziel*, Berlin 1928. See also Dartmann, p. 29.

96. See Mommsen, *From Weimar to Auschwitz*, p. 77.

97. The creation of works councils was combined with national trade union representation. Guillebaud, pp. 11–15.

98. This was the argument presented to the first regional Trade Union Congress in March 1946 by Hans Böckler, the head of the DGB in the British zone. See Dartmann, pp. 99–102. This analysis is supported by Hans Mommsen who writes that: 'The elimination of labour was an absolute requirement for the triumph of fascism . . . The fate of the Weimar Republic was only finally sealed when the belief gained ground that the SPD could be permanently excluded from political power and the Free and Christian Trades Union neutralised.' Mommsen, 'Class War of Codetermination', p. 67.

irrespective of party politics. The cumulative experience of organized labour during the Wilhelmine, Weimar and Nazi periods led to a distrust of the state as the representative of the common good.[99] In response they advanced the idea of a 'social' democracy, in which the governance of the economy was amenable to democratic negotiation.

Ordo-Liberalism

It is customary to assign the creation of the 'philosophical' framework of the 'social-market economy' to a group of economists associated with Freiburg University who described themselves as Ordo-Liberals.[100] Giersch writes that: 'In the Ordo liberal philosophy, which underlies the design of the West German Social-Market Economy, a thoroughgoing anti-trust and anti-cartel legislation has a central place.'[101] It is argued in the next chapter that the strictures of Ordo-liberalism concerning decartelization were ignored and economies of scale re-emerged as an important aspect of the German economy.[102] It is also argued that the emphasis given to currency reform and financial orthodoxy has been excessively emphasized in the explanation of subsequent export growth and productivity levels. Leszek Balcerowicz, the minister of finance and deputy prime minister of Poland in the Solidarity government of 1989–92, is representative of mainstream opinion when he writes in his article 'Common Fallacies in the Debate on the Economic Transition in Eastern Europe' that:

---

99. See Mommsen, 'State and Bureaucracy in the Brüning Era', in *From Weimar to Auschwitz*, pp. 79–118, p. 109.

100. The nomination of 'Ordo' liberalism was chosen by Walter Eucken (1891–1950), professor of economics at Freiburg University between 1929 and 1950, in order to evoke the medieval idea of a natural and harmonious order in society. He wrote: 'It was an order corresponding to the nature of man and the object, in which moderation and equilibrium prevail.' Walter Eucken, *Grundsätze der Wirtschaftspolitik*, Bern 1952, p. 372. The other leading social market theorists were Franz Böhm (1895–1977), Wilhelm Röpke (1899–1966), and Alexander Rüstow (1885–1963). For a comprehensive account of the biographies and ideas of the Ordo-liberals see Nicholls, pp. 32–121.

101. H. Giersch, H.H. Paqué and H. Schmeidling, *The Fading Miracle: Four Decades of Market Economy in Germany*, Cambridge 1993, p. 85 (hereafter Giersch).

102. See chapter three.

The term [social-market economy] was coined in Germany in the late 1940s by a group of liberal economists to describe a freely competitive capitalist economy with a certain admixture of social protection, but to a lesser degree than Sweden, for example.[103]

The argument presented in this section is that to describe the practices or the ideology of the social market as a 'freely competitive capitalist economy' is perhaps the most fundamental fallacy in the present debate on the transformation of Eastern Europe.

The social-market economy was described by each of its proponents as a 'third way' between what Erhard referred to as 'paleo-liberalism' identified with a market society and a centrally directed economy.[104] As such, the social-market economy is a residual third term opposed to state direction and self-regulating markets lacking any distinctive analytic categories or concepts of its own.[105] The idea of a 'third way', however, does capture an important aspect of the type of regime that emerged in West Germany, in which integration into the world economy was not accompanied by deregulated markets in labour and land.[106] As the ideas of 'liberal interventionism' and the 'third way' were coined by Wilhelm Röpke, this section will concentrate on his work.[107]

---

103. Leszek Balcerowicz, *Socialism, Capitalism and Transformation*, Budapest 1995, p. 223. At 19.4 per cent, the share of the net national product spent on welfare in 1953 was higher in Germany than in any other comparable country. In Sweden it was 13.5 and in Britain it was 12.5. See H.G. Hockerts, 'German Post-War Social Policies Against the Background of the Beveridge Plan', in W.J. Mommsen, ed., *The Emergence of the Welfare State in Britain and Germany*, London 1981 (hereafter Hockerts), p. 321.

104. Erhard developed its ideas into the idea of the 'formed' society (*formierte Gesellschaft*) which he opposed to a planned or a spontaneous order. It was the duty of the state, in this formulation, to prevent the 'proletarianization of the people' by a 'conscious cultivation of craft industries and small businesses'. See Nicholls, p. 155, p. 307. In the 'formed society' the institutions of the *Mittelstand* provide the framework of social life and are the precondition of a stable economic order.

105. This is the analysis presented in Rudolph Walther, who argues that the social-market economy is an 'opportunistic' concept with 'eclectic theoretical foundations' enjoying only the most distant connection with the meaning of 'liberalism'. 'Economic Liberalism', p. 201. See also Keith Tribe, 'Genealogy', pp. 203–40. Both articles were extremely helpful in the analysis made here.

106. For the first use of the term 'third way' see W. Röpke, *The Social Crisis of Our Time* (1942), Edinburgh 1950, pp. 4–38.

107. W. Röpke, *Die Lehre von der Wirtschaft*, Vienna 1937. W. Röpke, *International Economic Disintegration*, London 1942. W. Röpke, *Civitas Humana*, Edinburgh 1949.

The first assumption of Röpke's theory is that all economies are driven by need.[108] The second is that all economic activities require planning and a legitimate state to uphold rules of co-operation.[109] On this basis, he dismissed the argument that socialist economies are 'needs' based or that market economies are 'spontaneous'. The precondition of economic order, he argued, was a strong state which created the conditions for providing the stable expectations necessary for micro-economic planning. He distinguished between 'chaos', which resulted from state arbitrariness, and 'anarchy', which arose from decentralized economic decisions. He argued that the latter could only be achieved through a legitimate political order.[110] Röpke thus reversed the usual economic assumption that order emerges out of liberty by defending the proposition that political legitimacy is a precondition of economic freedom.[111] He argued that the greatest threat to political legitimacy, and therefore to economic order, was the cultural demoralization resulting from proletarianization.[112] Without strong state regulation and a society organized around values and institutions that do not reduce to personal advantage, the cultural and ethical practices upon which reliable co-operation depends would break down.[113] For this reason Röpke argued that: 'The capitalist impregnation of all sections of life in our society is a curse which we must banish, and the free expansion of the economy must not lead to the perversion of genuine human values.'[114]

The solution to proletarianization was institutional and required state support for those forces which retained 'vitally satisfying forms of life and work'.[115] Röpke's analysis of the failure of liberalism in the inter-war years was that economic dogma had rendered the state ineffectual in confronting social crisis and had thus ceded a rationality to communism and Fascism that he intended to rectify through his concept of 'liberal interventionism'.[116] In this the state

---

108. Röpke, *Die Lehre*, pp. 185–92.

109. Röpke, *Die Lehre*, p. 25.

110. Röpke, *Die Lehre*, p. 185.

111. See Tribe, 'Genealogy', p. 206.

112. Röpke, *Die Lehre*, pp. 166–70.

113. Röpke, *The Social Crisis of Our Time*, chapter one.

114. Röpke, *Die Lehre*, p. 190. Quoted in Nicholls, p. 96.

115. Röpke, *International Economic Disintegration*, p. 262.

116. W. Röpke, *German Commercial Policy*, London 1934, pp. 40–75. His argument is similar to that proposed by Polanyi, see chapter one, pp. 5–19.

would 'protect small and medium size property holdings, give support to independent farmers, break up industrial cities, revive pride in work and in professional standards, and combat the feeling of human rootlessness'.[117] This would achieve what he called a 'spontaneous order' that was not directed by the state but which preserved harmony between the institutions of society.[118] Röpke thus disputed the commonly held assumption of the Weimar period that large firms were necessarily more efficient than smaller-scale enterprises.[119] He argued that the number of small firms had increased in all industrial nations. Smaller firms were not only more flexible but the social costs of mass production were inordinately high. This led to the concentration of power which he argued was the core evil (Kernübel) of modern societies. Röpke thus called for a renewed emphasis on those groups who retained 'human scale' communities such as the small producer, the farmer, the artisan, the professional and the small shopkeeper. He urged land reform so that active workers could also be small-scale farmers. He wrote:

> The peasant world today presents, together with the sector of handicraft and other smaller branches outside agriculture, a last great island not yet inundated by mass society; hence we have still the solid rock of a form of human life and work which is inherently stable and vitally satisfying . . . It is an immeasurable benefit if this form still exists, as in the greatest part of continental Europe, and it is a great misfortune for a country if it has been destroyed, as in England, to such a degree that the loss is not even felt anymore.[120]

The preservation of private property and personal autonomy required active state intervention, not through directives or the setting of output targets, but through the institutional recognition of social groups and institutions which preserved an ethical

---

117. Röpke, Die Lehre, p. 190. See Nicholls, pp. 90–103.

118. The idea of 'harmony' between 'groups' is common to Erhard, Eucken and Röpke. Röpke explicitly drew upon Aquinas and Quadragesimo Anno in his analysis of the defects of market societies. See E.W.F. Dürr, Ordoliberalismus und Sozialpolitik, Winterthur 1954, p. 113.

119. See W. Röpke, 'Klein- und Mittelbetrieb in der Volkswirtschaft' in ORDO – Jahrbuch für die Ordnung von Wirtschaft und Gesellschaft, Vol. 1, 1948, pp. 155–74.

120. Röpke, International Economic Disintegration, p. 259.

orientation irreducible to self-advantage.[121] The third way would thus 'overcome the problems of proletarianization, mammoth industries, monopolies, the multifarious types of exploitation and the mechanizing effects of capitalist mass civilization'.[122] The means of achieving this was an increased role for the state in preserving 'forms of life' that were inhospitable to the rules of a contractual society.

The first principle of the social-market economy was consequently the protection of existing social institutions by the state as a defence against proletarianization. The second was the idea of equal opportunity (*Startgleichheit*). This was developed by Alexander Rüstow in his criticism of the inequalities generated by inheritance rights and his defence of progressive taxation.[123] He argued that only if there was an equal distribution of starting points could the autonomy necessary for effective participation in society be sustained.[124] The third was extensive retraining programmes for those who could not survive in their inherited 'form' of life.[125] Walter Eucken developed the argument that the state had an active role in providing incentives and establishing structures within the economy in pursuit of societal goals. Such measures could conform to the market as they did not take the form of directives. The outcome of economic activity could not be determined by the state, although the institutions of economic governance could be cultivated by the state through law. The market was considered as a structured process.[126]

The writings of Röpke, Erhard, Rüstow and Eucken are in most senses unremarkable. The conception of organic and non-contractual institutions which preserve a sense of place and belonging were part of the common coin of German social

---

121. Röpke, *The Social Crisis of Our Time*, p. 286.

122. Quoted in Nicholls, p. 98.

123. See his appendix to Röpke's *International Economic Disintegration*, pp. 277–83.

124. In this, the position of Ordo-liberalism is indistinguishable from the political liberalism of John Rawls. The fundamental idea is that the state subordinates the market in the name of individual autonomy. See chapter four, pp. 90–2.

125. Röpke, *The Social Crisis of Our Time*, pp. 354–90.

126. Walter Eucken, 'Die Wettbewerbsordnung und ihre Verwirklichung', in *ORDO - Jahrbuch für die Ordnung von Wirtschaft und Gesellschaft*, Vol. 2, 1949, pp. 381–98.

theory.[127] What is remarkable is that the social market is commonly cited as a significant ideological defence of the market order when its primary concern was with the preservation of institutions which protected society from the homogenization brought about by market sovereignty.

It has been argued in this chapter that a set of institutional practices embedded in daily working and religious life provided the ethical orientation which organized West German reconstruction. These were carried within the labour movement, Church and locality. No-one 'designed' post-war Germany, it was hewn out of far more durable and sophisticated moral and ethical materials than those provided by economic theory or any other social science methodology. The relationship between the market system, societal institutions, vocational organization, regional government and military constraints led to a 'spontaneous' order in which the goal of societal, and not simply market equilibrium, became the regulative ideal.[128] The order was spontaneous in that it did not conform to any design or blueprint. The British and Americans could impose neither their welfare nor economic system.[129] The idea of a societal equilibrium alluded to by Eucken, Röpke and Rüstow, was rooted in the philosophy and practices of the Catholic and labour movements. Economic activity was embedded within a self-organized society which imposed non-negotiable costs concerning democratic participation in economic decision-making and the necessity of negotiation. The ideologists of the social market provided a theory which allowed for agricultural protection, artisan practices, regional subsidies, recognized trade unions and myriad forms of state intervention. The vagueness of the ideology of the social-market economy is its most significant feature. It clouded the reality of societal restoration in the rhetoric of price reform. The legacy of its national political success has thus been the obscuring of institutional realities.

---

127. For an account of 'third way' thinking among the Kreisau group who organized the plot against Hitler, see Mommsen, *From Weimar to Auschwitz*, p. 214.

128. In this Ordo-liberalism was with the grain of Catholic and socialist thought.

129. See chapter three.

3

The Restoration of German Society

Land, Labour and Money

The central argument of this chapter is that if, following Polanyi, the extent to which land, labour and money are mobilized as commodities defines the 'form of integration' of economy and society, Germany is not a market society.[1] As regards land, agricultural production and housing have been subsidized and regulated irrespective of government since 1945. The price liberalization in 1948 omitted food prices and raw materials completely and agricultural protection doubled between 1950 and 1986.[2] The technique of using import quotas, subsidies, stockpiling and fixed grain rates was codified in the *Landswirtschaftsgesetz* of 1955 and subsequently incorporated into the Common Agricultural Policy of what is now the EU.[3]

Housing was also excluded from Erhard's price liberalization. Rents were set and held at the 1936 level and tenants in pre-1945 rent-controlled accommodation were guaranteed security of tenure.[4] The majority of houses built after 1950 were subsidized by

---

1. For the definition of 'form of integration' see chapter one, pp. 5–19.

2. For the Allied policy on agriculture see John E. Farquharson, *The Western Allies and the Politics of Food: Agricultural Management in Post-War Germany*, New Hampshire 1985. For details on the increases in agricultural tariffs after 1950 see Giersch, p. 111. For a list of the majority of prices which were excluded from Erhard's scheme see A.H. Hansonn, 'The 1948 West-German Economic Reforms: A Model for Eastern Europe?', Working Paper of the University of British Columbia No. 90-05, Vancouver 1990, p. 28. Also see Wolf, p. 37.

3. See Eric Owen Smith, *The German Economy*, London 1994, pp. 496–7 (hereafter Smith). The total agricultural subsidy in 1989 was DM 21 billion, 1 per cent of GDP.

4. See Smith, p. 389.

the government and regulated through the 1950 and 1956 House Construction Acts.[5] Half of these were administered by housing associations which were exempt from taxation and owned by the Church, unions and co-operative societies. The application of the subsidiarity principle in the administration of house-building should not disguise the scale of the subsidy.[6] The Equalization of Burdens Act of 1952 was, writes Hockerts:

> a programme of massive redistribution that was to benefit more than ten million refugees and people who had been bombed out. Several Acts were passed to look after the four million people who had been invalided, widowed or orphaned by the war. As about a third of the necessary housing was lacking, a building programme with massive subsidies from public funds was initiated.[7]

Some 54 per cent of investment in house-building between 1950 and 1954 was provided by the state, which increases to 60 per cent if the use of tax-deductible incentives is included.[8] Between 1953 and 1970 housing associations built over 69 per cent of new accommodation in West Germany.[9] The technical building of the projects was supervised by the *Heimstätten*, a non-profit institution which supervised quality control and gave advice and access to a skilled workforce, in which the artisan sector (Handwerk) played a vital role.[10] The owners of the houses were local authorities, banks, insurance companies and housing associations.[11] The

---

5. See Smith, p. 199.

6. See Hockerts, pp. 315–39, p. 317.

7. Hockerts, pp. 320–21. The Equalization of the Burdens Act was initially announced in 1948. See pp. 82–4.

8. See K.W. Roskamp, *Capital Formation in West Germany*, Michigan 1965, pp. 180–1. Also see Wendy Carlin, 'Economic Reconstruction in West-Germany: 1945–55: The Displacement of "Vegetative Controls"', in I.D. Turner, ed., *Reconstruction in Post-War Germany: British Occupation Policy and the Western Zones 1945–55*, Oxford 1989, pp. 37–65, p. 63 (hereafter Carlin).

9. See H. Tomann, 'The Housing Market, Housing Finance and Housing Policy in West Germany', *Urban Studies*, Vol. 27, No. 6, 1990, pp. 919–30.

10. The Handwerk performed the greatest proportion of work in housing and agriculture after 1945, fulfilling 88.7 per cent and 95.6 per cent of the contracts in these two sectors. See pp. 70–9.

11. Until its collapse in the late 1970s the trade union-owned *Neue Heimat* possessed 330,000 homes and controlled 240,000 others, making it the largest property company in Europe. Smith, p. 387.

needs of society were guaranteed by state transfer payments which facilitated the renewal of self-organized institutions.

As regards the status of the human being in the labour market, guaranteed rights of consultation and joint decision-making are institutionalized through the Co-determination Acts of 1951, 1952 and 1976.[12] Constraints on trade are maintained by craft and vocational institutions which administer the apprenticeship schemes and enforce quality control within the firm.[13] The public status of associations is further strengthened by parity supervision of the pension funds by the employers' associations and trade unions.[14] Collective bargaining is guaranteed by the Constitution at regional level and management's right to manage is not recognized in law.[15]

As concerns the commodity fiction of money, at no point was the deutschmark allowed to find its market price outside a guaranteed fixed rate.[16] The German Bundesbank was established in 1958 and its board remains comprised of elected representatives of the Federal States.[17]

The question of how West Germany could retain its international competitiveness, bearing in mind the decommodification of the countryside, the strong regulation of the housing market and the most 'inflexible' labour force in Western Europe, is one of the principal questions pursued here. The argument proposed is that by promoting trade unions with collective bargaining rights, enterprise democracy and a vocational training system based on apprenticeship, licensing and market restrictions, Germany has remained a viable industrial society. What the prevailing economic regime defines as vices are the basis of economic virtue. Economic success was based upon the preservation of a substantive society underpinned by non-market institutions with power in the economy.

---

12. See pp. 64–9.
13. See pp. 70–9.
14. See pp. 79–82.
15. See Wolfgang Streeck, 'Co-determination: After Four Decades', in *Social Institutions and Economic Performance: Studies of Industrial Relations in Advanced Capitalist Economies*, London 1992, pp. 137–69, pp. 157–8.
16. See C.B. Yenger, *International Monetary Relations*, New York 1976, pp. 494–5.
17. See Smith, pp. 8–12.

West Germany 1945

International consensus

The occupying powers in what was to become West Germany were France, Britain and the United States. The French state followed a political strategy which was to bear fruit in the iron and coal community and the development of a common agricultural policy which formed the protectionist origins of the EU.[18] The United States and Britain shared a notion of an international order in which Germany played a central role as the material and ideological barrier to Bolshevik advance. There were, however, fundamental differences between the two states concerning the type of social organizations that would characterize the new German society which were given by the dissimilarity between the ideologies of the two governments. Neither succeeded in imposing their national welfare or industrial systems on Germany. Competition and confusion between them, it will be argued, opened up the possibility for German society to develop its own distinctive institutions. It was within the often conflicting aspirations and directives of the occupation powers that internal German associations found the space to organize and redefine their identity and function within society.

The United States: federal politics and free markets

The United States emerged from the war with unprecedented reserves of military, political, economic and cultural capital which it sought to export as the author and enforcer of a new international system. It was the dominant military force, the possessor of the largest internal market, the most modern production techniques and the leading exporter of consumer goods.[19] The Federal Republic of Germany became the centrepoint of American designs concerning the reconstruction of Western Europe. The first US task was to define 'actual existing socialism' as a form of life worth rejecting. The communist threat, however, forced the

---

18. See Alan S. Milward, *The Reconstruction of Western Europe 1945–1951*, Berkeley 1984, chapter five.

19. See Arrighi, p. 275. In 1947 US gold reserves were 75 per cent of the world's total.

United States to take the trade unions in Western Europe far more seriously than they did in their other spheres of influence.[20] Those trade unions in Europe willing to endorse growth and productivity within the constraints of the 'New Deal' were seen as allies and, in Maier's words: 'Those who dissented were held to be regrettably partisan, obstructionist, and by 1947, subversive.'[21]

The second goal was to create a military alliance between Western European states that could contain Soviet power and retain US political and economic leadership in the region. The third was to establish non-corporatist but pro-corporate liberal democratic states based on principles of free trade and protected property rights.[22] This was expressed in US opposition to the establishment of works councils, co-determination and the continuation of Handwerk organizations in their zone.

Britain: Labour government and labour power

The British occupation was of a different order. A collectivist-oriented Labour Party had been elected in 1945. They proceeded with a policy of nationalization on a scale unequalled in any other Western European nation. Coal, steel, railways, gas, telecommunications, airlines and the Bank of England were all exclusively owned by the British state. The priority of public right was established in property development through the Town and Country Act of 1948.

The ideas of social order characteristic of the two active occupation regimes in Germany were thus substantially different. The British government was committed to an expansion of state power

---

20. See Carolyn Eisenberg, 'Working-Class Politics and the Cold War: American Intervention in the German Labour Movement, 1945-1949', *Diplomatic History*, Vol. 7, No. 4, 1983, pp. 283–306 (hereafter Eisenberg).

21. Charles S. Maier, 'The Politics of Productivity: Foundations of American International Policy after World War Two', in Peter J. Katzenstein, ed., *Between Power and Plenty: Foreign Economic Policies of Advanced Industrial States*, Wisconsin 1978, pp. 41–2. Maier charts the network of US-sponsored anti-Communist trade unions and the role that the AFL played in organizing counter insurgency against the CGL and CGT. CIA operative Thomas Braden estimated that $2 million was channelled to those unions which opposed left-wing organizations.

22. For a comprehensive analysis see E. Fones-Wolf, *Selling Free Enterprise*, Illinois 1995.

in both provision and production. The US viewed itself as an international global manager laying down the economic and political ground rules of post-war reconstruction. It is unsurprising, therefore, that Britain and the United States should diverge in their conception of the institutional character of West German society. The British Foreign Minister Ernest Bevin wrote in the Labour Party Review of International Politics:

> In the European scene . . . we are the last bastion of social democracy. It may be said that this now represents our way of life against the red tooth and claw of American Capitalism and the communist dictatorship of Soviet Russia.[23]

Their differences assumed significance, for the purposes of the argument developed here, in the conception they had of economic reconstruction and the space that was opened up for internal German agents. The organizations overseeing economic policy in the British zone co-operated with the unions and artisan organizations in developing new procedures in the sphere of non-state institutions.[24] The British administration provided a context within which vocational institutions in Germany could redefine their role in the German economy. Britain, as the occupier of the industrial region of the Rhine, could allow an autonomous policy in this zone only. It was the North Rhine Westphalia region, however, which served as the model that was adopted throughout West German society after 1949. The British zone supplied the political leadership of the two main parties, the trade unions, employers' associations and Handwerk, as well as the legal and institutional practices that formed the Federal Republic.[25]

National context and consensus

By September 1945 Germany was occupied by four foreign armies and bureaucracies. The identity of society had been altered by genocide, military losses, bombing, state repression and expulsions. A material context, however, remained in place. Factories existed, as did machine tools, skilled craftsmen, workers and

---

23. Quoted in Dartmann, p. 258.
24. See pp. 64–82.
25. See pp. 70–82.

managers.[26] The Nazis had modernized plant technology, rationalized production, standardized vocational training and increased the capacity for producing consumer goods.[27] Between 1938 and 1943 the stock of machine tools increased by 75 per cent, exceeding US capacity. By 1942 real investment in industrial production was two and a half times higher and capital stock was 60 per cent higher in 1945 than in 1936.[28] This investment was targeted towards the high technology and chemical firms which were to provide the foundation for post-war success.[29] Decartelization and reparations meant a depletion of capital stock of only 7 per cent. In capacity terms the German economy was in better shape in 1945 than it was in 1939. The existing capital stock was also serviceable as a high proportion of the workforce was employed in maintenance until production resumed.[30] The organizational demoralization and subsequent disintegration of society resulting from defeat posed more demanding problems than economic breakdown.[31]

Every aspect of German institutional life could be questioned as no institutions survived the war in an uncontested form. There was not a crisis of legitimacy so much as its absence. The country's borders had been redrawn and there were doubts as to

26. See Werner Abelshauser, *Wirtschaft in Westdeutschland 1945–1948. Rekonstruktion und Wachstumsbedingungen in der amerikanischen und britischen Zone*, Stuttgart 1975.

27. See Frederick L. McKitrick, 'Old World Craftsmen into Modern Capitalists: Artisans in Germany from National Socialism to the Federal Republic, 1939–1953', Doctoral Dissertation of the Faculty of Arts and Sciences, Columbia University 1994 (hereafter McKitrick), pp. 49–128. Also see John Gillingham, 'Industrial Apprenticeships and "Deproletarianisation": Labour Training in the Third Reich', *Central European History*, Vol. 18, 1985. See also section on Handwerk in this chapter.

28. See Carlin, pp. 39–42; Wolf, 'The Lucky Miracle', Table 2.1, p. 33. Wolf calculates that a net investment of 25.2 billion RM was counterbalanced after the war by 13.8 billion RM damage from bombing and a 2.8 billion depreciation resulting from decartelization and reparations leading to an 8.6 billion surplus. The use of slave labour also had a significant effect on the amount of surplus available for re-investment.

29. See Simon Reich, *The Fruits of Fascism: Post-war Prosperity in Historical Perspective*, New York 1990, pp. 60–5. For an analysis of this 'coincidence' see Carlin, p. 59.

30. Wolf, p. 52.

31. Wolf, p. 44.

whether it would continue to exist as a unified state. There were huge waves of immigration from the east which exacerbated claims on scarce resources, most particularly housing and raw materials.[32] There was the return of a defeated army, as well as widespread hunger, homelessness and a breakdown of the transport system.[33]

The structures of a war economy remained but the ownership of its assets was held exclusively by the occupying powers. The political parties were reliant on external licensing, funding and support. Social Democracy reconstituted itself with an organization and leadership that had changed considerably since its forced disbandment in May 1933.[34] The Christian Democratic Union was a new political organization. The trade unions, in what was to become West Germany, had been outlawed. The claims of large employers on existing industrial assets were uncertain.[35] Handwerk had prospered under Nazi rule and the state administration had lost much of its reputation for impartiality.[36] The army was defeated and the police disgraced. Of the two churches Lutheranism was

---

32. Seven and a half million refugees arrived in West Germany between 1945 and 1948. A further four and a half million arrived between 1949 and 1955. Many of the new arrivals were skilled workers, and while this was ultimately a great asset, the majority of arrivals were initially housed in temporary accommodation in the countryside and were thus unavailable for industrial work. See Werner Abelshauser, 'The Economic Policy of Ludwig Erhard', EUI Working Paper, Florence 1984, p. 12. For the beneficial effects of the arrival of the refugees see R.E.H. Mellor, *The Two Germanies: A Modern Geography*, London 1974, p. 149.

33. For the extent of this see J. Gimbel, *The American Occupation of Germany: Politics and the Military 1945-49*, Stanford 1968, p. 35. For the breakdown of the transport system see Abelshauser, *Wirtschaft*, p. 152. Only 1,000 out of 13,000 kilometres of track were usable, 60 per cent of the rolling stock was broken and a third of the rest was damaged. See also Wolf, p. 51.

34. See A. Glees, *Exile Politics During the Second World War: The Social Democrats in Britain*, Oxford 1982.

35. The Federation of German Employers' Associations or *Bundesvereinigung Deutscher Arbeitgeberverbände* (BdA) was formed in 1949 and adopted a far more conciliatory approach to the unions than its Weimar predecessor the VdA. See Ronald F. Bunn, 'The Federation of German Employers' Associations: A Political Interest Group', *Western Political Quarterly*, Vol. 13, No. 3, 1960, pp. 652–69.

36. For an account of the traditional high-standing of the national administration see Hans Mommsen, 'State and Bureaucracy in the Brüning Era', *From Weimar to Auschwitz*, pp. 79-118.

considerably more compromised than Catholicism.[37] With the Protestant ascendancy lost through the Soviet occupation of Prussia, this was to prove of considerable political importance. The internal dissolution of society was complemented by the external domination by the Allied armies which took on a confused and ultimately adversarial form.

The Role of Solidarity, Subsidiarity and Status in the Re-constitution of German Society

Co-determination

Co-determination (*Mitbestimmung*) refers to the participation of works councils in the administration of the firm, equal responsibilities between unions and employers in the management of pension funds, and the representation of trade unions and elected employees on the board of directors.[38] Within each enterprise with more than six employees there is a legal right to elect a works council entitled to information, consultation and managerial authority concerning personnel policy and the setting of overtime.[39] There are two forms of board-room representation. The first was formalized in the Co-determination Act of 1951 which established parity representation on the supervisory boards for employees and employers.[40] This applied exclusively to the coal,

---

37. For an analysis of the relationship between the Lutheran Church and National Socialist ideology see S. Heschel, 'Nazifying Christian Theology: Walter Grundmann and the Institute for the Study and Eradication of Jewish Influence on German Church Life', *Church History*, Vol. 63, No. 4, 1994. The credibility of the Catholic Church was reinforced by their role in dealing with the influx of refugees. See Ian Connor, 'The Churches and the Refugee Problem in Bavaria 1945–1949', *Journal of Contemporary History*, Vol. 20, 1985, pp. 399–421.

38. German companies are legally compelled to have two boards, a management board (*Vorstand*) responsible for the direct administration of the firm and a supervisory board (*Aufsichtsrat*) made up of stockholders and workers, the main task of which is the appointment of managers and the development of enterprise strategy. See Dartmann, p. 9.

39. Dartmann, p. 78.

40. The supervisory board consisted of eleven people, five from Labour (two nominated by the worker councils, two by the national unions and one commonly agreed external candidate), and five from Capital (three members appointed by the owners, one from the industrial federation and an external appointee). The eleventh member and chairman had to be agreed by both sides and was usually the local mayor.

iron and steel industries. Outside these industries the Works Constitution Act of 1952 (*Betriebsverfassungsgesetz*) stated that in all companies with over five hundred employees, a third of the seats on the supervisory and management boards had to be allocated to members of the workforce. This formalized an arrangement that had been negotiated by the trades unions and employers' association within the British zone between 1946 and 1948.[41]

Allied policy toward the trade unions

In October 1945 the IG Farben concern was put under Allied control. By November the British had taken control of Krupps and in December the coal-mining industry was sequestrated. By 1946, with their seizure of the Hermann Göring and Vereinigte Stahlwerke, Britain gained control of the largest iron, steel and coal producers in Europe.[42] In none of these cases was there a notion of returning these industries to their previous owners.[43] In April 1946 the North German Iron and Coal Control issued a Works Council Law establishing parity representation on the supervisory boards of each of the iron, coal and steel enterprises under their control, while mandating the establishment of works councils.[44] The importance of organized labour was recognized by the British bureaucracy directly concerned with industrial policy. In 1945, the head of the North German Iron and Steel Control, Harris Burland, declared that trade unions were: 'one of the chief stabilising influences in the political, social and economic life of the British zone'.[45]

Co-determination was subsequently extended to all the pre-war

---

41. See Dartmann, p. 12
42. Dartmann, p. 28.
43. Law No. 152 of the British Military Government declared that all industrial assets under its control were liable to 'confiscation, direction, administration, supervision or other controls'. See Parnell, p. 81.
44. This was argued, by the trade unions and the British, to be in accordance with Article 12 of the Potsdam Agreement which stipulated that German industry was to be decartelized, and 'excessive' economic concentration of ownership and power eliminated. Dartmann, p. 78. German coal prices were directly regulated by the Allies until 1956.
45. Dartmann, p. 22. In the same declaration in which parity worker representation on the supervisory boards was authorized, bankers were excluded. The priority of production to the disciplines of finance was established.

cartels of the Montan sector of iron, coal and steel.[46] The trade-union representative on the management board was made the labour director and parity was established on the supervisory boards of each company.

Events in the US zone took a different course. The State Department was extremely concerned about the spontaneous establishment of works councils and their links to the trade unions. Louis A. Wiesner, the State Department labour specialist, wrote that: 'to foster this formation (works councils) in preference to and as a basis for trade unions seems to be a gratuitous invitation to German workers to recall their revolutionary traditions'.[47] In the American zone trade unions were thus barred from participating in collective bargaining beyond the plant and works councils were disqualified from managerial decisions involving economic questions.

A social democracy: co-determination and the labour movement

Some 90 per cent of Germany's energy needs were satisfied by coal production before 1945 and this increased immediately afterwards.[48] The pattern of industrial relations in the Montan sector was of primary importance in reactivating German industry and establishing the relations of production in the new Republic. Abelshauser writes that:

> Lacking virtually all other basic raw materials and isolated from the world market, Germany was more dependent upon coal than most other industrial countries. In fact, coal was the backbone of all German industry.[49]

The employers' association recognized what was at stake and mounted a campaign against the continuation of co-determination.[50] The Bi-zonal Economics Council, chaired by Erhard,

---

46. See Dartmann, p. 89.

47. See Eisenberg, p. 286.

48. See John R. Gillingham, *Industry and Politics in the Third Reich: Ruhr Coal, Hitler and Europe*, New York 1985, p. 49.

49. Abelshauser, 'Economic Policy of Ludwig Erhard', p. 14

50. See Ronald F. Bunn, 'The Ideology of the Federation of German Employers' Associations', *American Journal of Economics and Sociology*, Vol. 18, No. 4, 1959, pp. 369–79. Dartmann, pp. 164–98.

pressed for the restoration of Weimar company law which would have rendered co-determination illegal. In April 1947 the miners went on hunger strike over the threat to co-determination and the SPD resigned from its participation in the Council.[51] Despite the opposition of the employers, the practices established in the British zone prevailed. After 1949 Adenauer's government supported co-determination and passed the 1951 and 1952 Acts.[52]

In 1976 the Works Constitution Act strengthened the responsibilities of works councils in the setting of piece rates, the design of workplaces and all matters concerning promotion and retraining. It accorded works councils greater production-level control over overtime and strengthened arbitration procedures in cases of dismissal, which were characterized by a high level of severance payment, retraining offers and relocation expenses.[53] Wage levels were set through regional collective bargaining with recourse of strike action. Parity representation between employers and employees in the control of pension funds was established in all sectors of the economy.[54]

The German High Court ruled in 1982 that co-determination took priority over the claims of shareholders as it was a matter of 'public good' and this overruled the civil law concerning the ownership of capital by joint-stock companies.[55] By redistributing rights and duties within the firm the relations between management and workforce became a matter of negotiation as national unions gained a knowledge of economic performance and a practical role

---

51. Dartmann, pp. 107–19.

52. See chapter two, pp. 34–43.

53. Before an employee is given notice an employer has to inform the works council or the dismissal is void (Sec. 102 of the Betriebwerfassunggesetz). If the works council contradicts the employer's decision, the matter goes to arbitration. A worker can only be dismissed if after a retraining programme they are judged not to have the personal capacity to fulfil the responsibility of their new role. If this is not the case employment is continued. Should the worker agree to leave, they receive twelve months severance at full pay. See Eric Schanze and Karl-Heinz Haunhorst, 'Security of Tenure in Conventional and "Flexible" Employment regimes – A Neo-Institutional Perspective', paper presented at the conference Labour Market Institutions and Constraints, EUI Florence, May 1993. For the level of severance pay in the mining industry see Parnell, p. 121.

54. Smith, p. 206.

55. See Streeck, 'Co-determination after Four Decades', pp. 137–69.

in the management of the economy.[56] Incentives were not only linked to wages but to the development of industry based on shared knowledge of the conditions and constraints which confronted each company and sector.[57] This was strengthened through the organization of pensions and the democratic administration of their funds. This led to less resistance to technological change and greater flexibility in accepting retraining and a reallocation of responsibility.[58] The sacrifices expected of workers were balanced by their participation in the process of production as an institutional partner.

Through the establishment of co-determination, four institutional spheres of negotiation were established between capital and labour concerning the governance of the economy. The most immediate is the firm-level works councils in which conflict is resolved through third-party arbitration. At the regional level collective bargaining is guaranteed by the Constitution and is characterized by the strike sanction. The third level is the firm's board of directors, in which conflict can only be resolved by negotiation. Democratic parity administration of the pension funds by the trade unions and the Employers' Federation strengthens the incentive to pursue the common good of the sector through the link established in the 1957 Pensions Act between present wage levels and the rate of pension payment.[59]

The four institutional levels of obligatory co-operation are characterized by different patterns of conflict and negotiation. It was argued in chapter one that markets require a substantive society characterized by non-rationalistic institutions in order to generate the goods necessary for its sustainable survival. These include a physical environment, skills and levels of trust that a society based exclusively on the immediate maximization of profits has difficulty generating. The production of goods requires the participation of non-market institutions in the economy if the

---

56. This idea has recently been defended by Samuel Bowles and Herbert Gintis, 'A Political and Economic Case For The Democratic Enterprise', *Economics and Philosophy*, Vol. 9, 1993, pp. 75–100.

57. See Stephen C. Smith, 'On the Economic Rationale for Co-determination Law', *Journal of Economic Behaviour and Organisation*, Vol. 16, 1991, pp. 261–81.

58. See I. Maitland, *The Causes of Industrial Disorder: A Comparison of a British and German Factory*, London 1983.

59. See pp. 79–82.

consumption of goods is not to deplete the cultural, ethical and environmental resources necessary for its reproduction. This requires the continued vitality of values that contradict the assumptions of the market concerning reciprocity, trust and knowledge. This, it was argued, requires democratic institutions embedded in the economy based upon protecting the status of nature, labour and the productive organizations of society.[60] In short, in order for an economy to flourish, values antithetical to self-interest are required to play a constitutive role in productive activities. The relationship between these organizations and those based on the immediate maximization of profit, of necessity, is conflictual. If this were not the case, the institutions would be unable to preserve the conditions necessary for the production of goods. The most significant tension in contemporary societies, it was argued, is between the substantive practices of production and the unconstrained enforcement of managerial prerogative.

Co-determination retains the necessity of conflict through regional collective bargaining and works council arbitration. It also institutionalizes common interests in the future welfare of the sector and the enterprise through parity control of pension funds and substantial representation in the boardroom. Regional collective bargaining ensures that differentials are narrowed and wages kept high, thus precluding low cost solutions to competitive pressure.[61] The incentive to invest in skills as a source of competitive advantage is increased by the difficulty in sacking workers without the approval of the works council. This leads to a further reliance on an effective national system of vocational training. Co-determination ensures that the trade unions have full information and the institutional power to negotiate enterprise and sectoral survival strategies. These limitations on managerial prerogative concerning strategy, job-definition and the organization of production provided the cultural resources which facilitated the capacity for effective adaptation to market changes without sacrificing productive capacity.

---

60. See chapter one, pp. 5–19.
61. Streeck, 'Productive Constraints', p. 40.

Handwerk[62]

Marx was representative of nineteenth-century opinion when he wrote that artisans would 'sink gradually into the proletariat' as their capital was too small to compete with industry and their skills were rendered redundant by technological innovation.[63] The collapse into the proletariat, however, never happened. The proportion of the population employed in the artisan economy in Germany rose from 45 per 1000 in 1894, to 60 in 1926 and to 80 by 1966.[64] By the late 1970s, 15.5 per cent of all employed persons in the Federal Republic worked in the Handwerk sector.[65] It contributed 11 per cent of GNP compared to 8.3 per cent in 1936.[66] In 1985 53 per cent of sixteen to nineteen year olds were educated in its vocational training scheme.[67] In terms of productivity gains, Handwerk have also kept pace with industry.[68] As the market for customized quality goods continues to grow,

---

62. The term Handwerk will be used here to designate the artisans' chambers and the guilds, the institutions which represent the artisan trades and enforce their rights, while the term Handwerker refers to the master craftsman. For an outstanding account of the Handwerk organisation in Germany see McKitrick. I would like to thank the author for allowing me access to his, as yet, unpublished research, and also to thank Allan Silver for tracing the author. Much of the argument made in this section draws upon McKitrick's research. See also Wolfgang Streeck, 'The Logics of Associative Action and the Territorial Organisation of Interests: The Case of German Handwerk', in *Social Institutions and Economic Performance*, pp. 105–36.

63. For an account of shared assumptions concerning modernization and increased economies of scale see Sable and Zeitlin, 'Historical Alternatives'. Bernstein, as an aspect of the revisionist critique of Marxism, argued that Handwerk had an economic rationality and an established place in advanced capitalist economies. See Eduard Bernstein, *Die Voraussetzungen des Sozialismus und die Aufgaben der Sozialdemokratie*, Stuttgart 1920, p. 98.

64. Wilhelm Wernet, *Handwerkspolitik*, Göttingen 1972, p. 77.

65. In 1990 Handwerk companies employed 12 million persons, two-thirds of all private sector employees. McKitrick, p. 395.

66. See Heinrich August Winkler, 'Stabilisierung durch Schrumpfung: Der gewerbliche Mittelstand in der Bundesrepublik', in Werner Conze and M. Rainer Lepsius, eds, *Sozialgeschichte der Bundesrepublik Deutschland*, Stuttgart 1983, p. 188.

67. See B. Casey, 'The Dual Apprenticeship System and the Recruitment and Retention of Young Persons in West Germany', *British Journal of Industrial Relations*, Vol. 24, No. 4, 1986, pp. 63–81.

68. McKitrick writes that 'Over the period 1949–1961 Handwerk sales rose 330% which exceeded that of industry by 15%.' McKitrick, p. 409.

industry is increasingly reliant on Handwerk to supply tools, machinery and parts according to individual specifications which enables firms to switch production type quickly.[69] In 1983 Handwerk represented 496,000 firms, 3.9 million employees and had double the combined turnover of the chemical and motor industries.[70]

Chambers, guilds and vocational training

There are two Handwerk institutions, the chambers (*Kammern*) and the guilds (*Innungen*). The chambers represent all artisans, enforce apprenticeship laws, administer the vocational training system and distribute masters licences. The Master's Certificate of Competency requires a seven-year apprenticeship culminating in the production of a masterpiece and the passing of theoretical exams which include accounting, tax law and marketing courses. Any firm practising recognized artisan trades without the appropriate accreditation is liable to prosecution by the chambers.[71] These trades range from chimney-sweep to precision optician, carpenter to orthopaedic shoe-maker, butcher to publisher, car mechanic to neon-sign producer.[72] What legally defines Handwerk is not the size of the firm but the role of skilled labour in the internal organization of production which has to be 'sizeable and dominant'.[73]

The chambers are also responsible for vocational training which provides the ideology and the organizational structure of Handwerk institutions.[74] The importance of vocational training is defended at two levels. The first is that small firms are more likely to survive in competition with industry if their skills are of a higher quality. The second argument concerns the overall performance of the economy and the role that Handwerk training plays in

---

69. For the effect that 'national skill formation' has on the performance of economies see Sorge and Streeck, pp. 19–47. See also chapter one, pp. 19–28.

70. See Streeck, 'Logics of Associative Action', p. 106.

71. The Gesetz zur Ordnung des Handwerks of 1953 subdivided artisan trades into seven sectors: building and construction; metal; wood-work; clothing, textile and leather; food; health and body care; and glass, paper and ceramics.

72. For a full list of the trades see McKitrick, pp. ix–xv.

73. See Streeck, 'Logics of Associative Action', p. 111.

74. Between 1970 and 1983, 397,000 young artisans were trained at the rate of 28,000 a year.

supplying skilled workers to industry.[75] The supply of skilled labour to industry has formed the basis of Handwerk's justification of its privileged market position and the powers of self-government accorded to it within the economy.[76] Local chambers have the power to determine whether a firm is suitable to train apprentices and withdraw a firm's training licence if this is not the case. This imposes public surveillance on work practices and ensures conformity to quality norms.[77] Vocational training in Germany is thus publicly regulated and vocationally administered. This ensures that virtue is institutionally protected within the economy through the public status of self-governing institutions which guard against short-term advantage undermining the provision of personally supervised and trained workers as public goods.

Each firm invests substantial amounts in training workers who are free to leave for better jobs.[78] It is because other firms are constrained to do the same that an individual cost to each firm becomes a public good through the securing of a collective supply of qualified personnel to the region.[79] The training by Handwerker firms is complemented by attendance of mandatory courses at the *Berufschulen*, or vocational schools.[80] Some 73 per cent of the costs of vocational training are met by the firm, with the state

75. The training system adopted in the industrial sector in the 1970s was consciously modelled on the adoption of a three-year apprenticeship and the opportunity for skilled workers to become an *Industrie-Meister*. See B. Mahnkopf, 'The "Skill-Oriented" Strategies of German Trade Unions: Their Impact on Efficiency and Equality Objectives', *British Journal of Industrial Relations*, Vol. 30, No. 1, 1992, pp. 61–82.

76. For an analysis of the meaning of sectoral self-government (*Selbstverwaltung*) and the role that Public Law Status plays in its organization see Parnell, pp. 92–7.

77. See W. Franz and D. Soskice, 'The German Apprenticeship System', Working Paper FSO 94-302, Wissenschaftszentrum Berlin für Sozialforschung, Berlin 1994.

78. See D. Harhoff and T.J. Kane, 'Financing Apprenticeship Training: The Evidence from Germany', Working Paper of the National Bureau of Economic Research, No. 4557, Massachusetts 1993. Also see W. Franz and D. Soskice, 'The German Apprenticeship System', Working Paper FSO 94-302, Wissenschaftszentrum Berlin für Sozialforschung, Berlin 1994.

79. Hirst, 'Flexible Specialization', p. 42. Also see David Soskice, 'Reconciling Markets and Institutions: The German Apprenticeship System', in L. Lynch, ed., *Training and the Private Sector: International Comparisons*, Chicago 1993.

80. See Wolfgang Streeck, *The Role of the Social Partners in Vocational Training and Further Training*, Berlin 1987.

contributing the remainder.[81] By 1993 Handwerker provided nearly 500,000 apprenticeship places.

Guilds, in contrast to the Chambers which represent all Handwerker within their region, represent specific local trades.[82] Although guild membership is voluntary, 85–90 per cent of eligible firms have elected to join. The primary responsibility of the guilds is to provide insurance in which employers and workers cover the costs equally.[83] There are incentives to virtue.

> Since absenteeism is lower in artisanal firms than in large industrial enterprises, the percentage of the wage charged by the guild insurance fund is also lower. Membership of these funds is open only to employers that belong to the respective guilds.[84]

It was argued in chapter one that firms and individuals will invest in the public good of 'human capital formation' only if the cost is shared and if they are afforded exemption from public bads such as low-cost labour and cut-price competition in the product market. The Handwerk organizations offer this protection.

The preservation of status

Resistance to proletarianization through the preservation of skilled status in the economy is the link between each historical stage of Handwerk development.[85] Handwerk had begun to decline in the sixteenth century and by 1800 average income was one-third of its level three hundred years earlier.[86] The encroachment of the centralized state and the national market steadily eroded guild authority which was finally broken by the Stein-Hardenberg reforms of 1810–11 in which Handwerk corporations were deprived of their organizational authority to restrict entrance to

---

81. D. Sandowski, 'The Finance and Governance of the German Apprenticeship System', *Journal of Institutional and Theoretical Economics*, Vol. 137, No. 2, pp. 234–51.

82. McKitrick, p. 151.

83. See Smith, p. 219.

84. Streeck, 'Logics of Associative Action', p. 117.

85. See Noyes, *Organisation and Revolution*, pp. 77–127, Barrington Moore, *Injustice*, p. 160. McKitrick, p. 34.

86. See Wilhelm Abel, *Massenarmut und Hungerkrisen im vorindustriellen Deutschland*, Göttingen 1972.

trades or set standards of production.[87] In 1871 freedom of trade (*Gewerbefreiheit*) was extended from the North German confederation to the entire territory of the newly formed Reich.[88] This was resisted by Handwerk and in alliance with peasants, large landowners and industry, a series of laws were passed in the 1880s which restored their corporate status.[89] The law of 1897 provided that the Handwerk could establish their own Chambers and the law of 1908 established the Minor Certificate of Competency (*Kleine Befähigungsnachweis*) which stipulated that only licensed masters could train apprentices.[90]

During the First World War the guilds and chambers assumed the task of procuring wartime orders and distributing the raw materials necessary for their fulfilment.[91] Guild membership rose substantially and the number of co-operatives doubled. These were organized by the Chambers in order to provide the economies of scale required for competing with large firms.[92] During the period of the Weimar Republic, however, Handwerk were threatened first by inflation and then by the subsequent stabilization policy during which many artisans lost their savings and their status. While the period immediately after 1920 marked an increase in prosperity, by 1932 Handwerker took home half of their 1928 earnings.[93] In 1932, 17 per cent of national bankruptcies were of Handwerk businesses. There was disproportionate support for Nazism among Protestant Handwerker while Catholic artisans generally supported the Centre Party.[94]

---

87. For a summary of government legislation on free trade and Handwerk restrictions see Rudolph Stadelmann and Wolfram Fischer, *Die Bildungswelt des Deutschen Handwerkers um 1800: Studien der Soziologie des Kleinbürgers im Zeitalter Goethes*, Berlin 1955.
88. See Peter John, *Handwerk im Spannungsfeld zwischen Zunftordnung und Gewerbefreiheit*, Cologne 1987, pp. 284–5.
89. McKitrick, p. 10.
90. McKitrick, p. 17.
91. See J Kocka, 'The First World War and the *Mittelstand*: German Artisans and White Collar Workers', *Journal of Contemporary History*, No. 8, 1973, pp. 100–23.
92. J. Kocka, *Facing Total War: German Society 1914–1918*, Leamington Spa 1984, p. 40.
93. See Rembart Untersted, *Mittelstand in der Weimarer Republik: Die Soziale Entwicklung und Politische Orientierung von Handwerk, Kleinhandel und Hausbesitz, 1919–1937*, Frankfurt 1989.
94. See M.H. Katter, *The Nazi Party, A Social Profile of Members and Leaders*

In contrast to the trade unions, which were abolished and their leaders imprisoned, the Nazis passed three laws which strengthened the recognition of Handwerk in the economy. The First Decree of 15 June 1934 defined seventy-two trades which could be legally practised as Handwerk, thus settling boundary disputes with industry while making guild membership obligatory.[95] The *Führerprinzip* became the selection procedure for leadership and a court of honour (*Ehrengerichtsbarkeit*) was established to adjudicate offences including unfair competition and the cheating of customers. In January 1935 the leadership principle was extended to the chambers. The Nazis also granted the most sought after Handwerk goal since 1848, the Major Certificate of Competency (*Große Befähigungsnachweis*). According to this law, only those Handwerker who had received their masters title would be permitted to practise their craft. The masters title was granted by the Chambers and was received at the end of a course of training, the details of which were incorporated into the 1953 Law. The curriculum and examination were set and administered by the Chambers which were established as corporations with a public law status.

The Nazis also pursued a policy of 'co-ordination' between Handwerk and industry.[96] They did not limit competition and there was no attempt to control prices until 1938. Corporate legislative bodies were not established. The number of one-man shops was drastically reduced as a shift to repair, installation and maintenance was pursued.[97] In 1943 Handwerk representatives were drafted onto the main committees of economic planning and the number of trades under their jurisdiction increased.[98] Handwerk, as was the case with industry, was in a stronger position at the end of the Third Reich than it was at the beginning. The surviving shops were more productive, the relationship with industry less

---

1919-1945, Cambridge 1983, pp. 23–4. For the movement of Handwerker from the liberal parties to the Nazis see Heinrich August Winkler, 'From Social Protection to National Socialism: The German Small Business Movement in Comparative Perspective', *Journal of Modern History*, Vol. 48, 1976, pp 7–8.

95. See Bernhard Keller, *Das Handwerk im faschistischen Deutschland*, Cologne 1980.

96. McKitrick, p. 41.

97. McKitrick, p. 94.

98. McKitrick, p. 119.

antagonistic and Handwerk organizations had a functional role in training, procuring contracts and organizing co-operatives.

Allied policy toward Handwerk

The breakdown of central government after 1945 led to an immediate reliance on local institutions. The first free and secret elections in Germany since 1932 were held to elect the leadership of the guilds and the chambers in the town of Aachen in January 1945.[99] The dilemma facing Handwerk was that of how to present their 'traditional' practices as something other than Nazi innovations of no more than a decade's duration. Britain and the US pursued opposed policies.

In June 1946 the British instructed the German Economic Advisory Board (*Zentralamt für Wirtschaft*) to prepare a report on basic questions of social organization which recommended the democratization and preservation of Handwerk institutions.[100] On 6 December the British passed an ordinance confirming the certificate of competency and the status of Handwerk chambers as public law corporations.[101] It abolished the leadership principle, obligatory guild membership and the Handwerk courts of honour, while mandating democratic election procedures and introducing co-determination. One-third of chamber membership and their executive committee were to consist of deputies elected by journeymen who had previously enjoyed no democratic rights.[102] By the end of 1946, Handwerk's status had been restored and its democratic structures expanded in the British zone.

In the American zone of Bavaria, Hesse and Baden-Württemberg developments took a different course. The US were committed to a multi-lateral free trade in which all German restrictive practices

99. McKitrick, p. 150.

100. Its chairman was the SPD representative Viktor Agartz. See Detlef Perner, 'Die "Reorganisation" der Handwerkskammern in der britischen Besatzungszone nach 1945' in Dietmar Petzina and Walter Euchner, eds, *Wirtschaftspolitik im britischen Besatzungsgebiet 1945–1949*, Düsseldorf 1984. See also pp. 64–9.

101. McKitrick, p. 192. This is in contrast to their treatment of the employers' corporation, the *Industrie- und Handelskammern*, which was abolished in the British zone and made an entirely voluntary organization. See Dartmann, p. 86.

102. See Detlef Perner, *Mitbestimmung im Handwerk? Die politische and soziale Funktion der Handwerkskammern im Geflecht der Unternehmerorganisationen*, Cologne 1983.

were to be removed.[103] In November 1948, the US Military Government stripped Handwerk of its corporate status and powers of self-administration.[104] The certificate of competency was also eliminated with the exception of those trades designated necessary for 'public health, safety and welfare'. In this case the qualifications of the candidates were to be judged directly by the state.[105]

The Handwerk response to the abolition of their status in the US zone was to argue that their organizations performed a regulatory function which would otherwise have to be assumed by the state. Handwerk presented themselves as a democratic alternative to state centralization and, explicitly drawing upon Röpke's ideas, argued that the concentration of power in the state could only be counterbalanced by a de-concentration of power in society.[106] At a time of scarcity and black-market dealing, the Handwerk claimed to uphold an 'ethos' and commitment to honesty that played a crucial role in protecting the public from cheating.[107] Handwerk presented themselves as a diverse and decentralized organization and thus not subject to the Potsdam accords on decartelization and the removal of 'excessive concentration of economic power'.[108]

Partly in response to the US claim that Handwerk used their institutions to protect artisans against improvements in production and marketing techniques, the leadership of Handwerk after 1945 pushed for rationalization and proper book-keeping.[109] The means by which technical help and assistance was disseminated was through local business support bureaus run by the chambers. Economies of scale were encouraged through the further development of co-operatives. These took the form of purchasing, marketing and productive co-operatives which were particularly effective in the building trades when bidding for large contracts. Credit co-operatives were established which give small businesses

103. See Volker Bergahn, *The Americanization of German Industry 1945–1973*, New York 1986, pp. 33–9.

104. See Gimbel, *The American Occupation*, pp. 237–8. McKitrick, p. 251.

105. McKitrick, p. 248.

106. McKitrick, p. 386.

107. The low level of black market activity, given the conditions in 1945, does need explanation. Less than 10 per cent of economic transactions took place outside legal channels. See H. Manderhausen, 'Prices, Money and the Distribution of Goods in Post-war Germany' *American Economic Review*, Vol. 39, 1949, pp. 646–72.

108. McKitrick, p. 240.

109. McKitrick, p. 270.

access to investment capital at favourable rates of interest.[110] The authority to supervise matters vital to the existence of every firm lent further legitimacy and prestige to Handwerk organizations after 1945. A compulsory system of schooling was introduced by the Chambers as a necessary condition for receiving a masters licence which taught business management, legal and tax systems and cost accounting.[111] Their legal status gave them the power to ensure that the new generation of Handwerker were equipped with the skills necessary to operate a capitalist firm.[112] The Handwerk 'tradition' articulated after 1945 was developed as a justification for democratic vocational organizations with coercive power in the economy. This could only be effective if the Handwerk institutions could present themselves as playing a rational role in the economy and providing necessary protection and services to artisans. The reform of the chambers and the guilds after 1945 achieved both.

One of the reasons for the durability of Handwerk lies in the redefinition of its function and a realignment of its ideology.[113] The emergence and permanence of industry led to the development of a Handwerk response based upon the modernization of production and the rationality of sectoral self-administration and reciprocal self-help.[114] There has been a decline in the one man shop and an increase in firm size which has fallen steadily from 75 per cent of all Handwerk in 1875 to 17.7 per cent in 1977.[115] There is an average of eight employees per firm, 26 per cent of whom were employed in enterprises of more than fifty employees.[116] New trades in electronics, radio, television, gas, water, heating, cooling and ventilation were legally recognized and the older declining

---

110. McKitrick, p. 423.

111. McKitrick, p. 271.

112. See Streeck, 'Logics of Associative Action', p. 115.

113. For the view that emphasizes the progressive aspects of Handwerk ideology and practice see Adelheid von Saldern, 'The Old *Mittelstand* 1890–1933: How "Backward" Were the Artisans?', *Central European History*, Vol. 25, No. 1, 1992, pp. 27–51. For the view which stresses the 'reactionary' and 'feudal' aspects of the Handwerk tradition see Shulamit Volkov, *The Rise of Popular Anti-modernism in Germany: The Urban Master Artisans 1873-1896*, Princeton 1978, p. 328.

114. See Dirk Georges, *Handwerk und Interessenpolitik: Von der Zunft zur modernen Verbandsorganisation*, Frankfurt 1993, pp. 29–37.

115. McKitrick, p. 404.

116. Winkler, *Mittelstand*, pp. 188–9.

trades such as shoe and watchmakers are now almost exclusively oriented towards repair.[117]

It has been argued in this section that Handwerk have played an important role in framing the 'rate of change' and maintaining the 'form of integration' of economy and society in each stage of modern German history.[118] Within Handwerk, tradition and innovation were combined to produce new institutional practices that incorporated changes in productive techniques, technology, marketing and accounting within the framework premised upon the preservation of craftsmanship. The ideological affinity of Handwerk and the CDU after 1945 was extensive. They shared respect for small private property and an opposition to collectivism. Catholic social teaching and Handwerk shared a critique of industrial capitalism in that the standardized manufacture of homogeneous items for anonymous markets appealed to neither.[119] The passage of the Handwerk Ordinance of 1953 by the Bundestag adopted the British 1946 Ordinance and a stronger role for Handwerk in the governance of the German economy than at any other period in modern German history.

Pensions

The way in which solidarity, subsidiarity and status functioned through the establishment of democratic sectoral self-government is demonstrated in the administration of pensions. The welfare system initiated by Bismarck devolved the greatest part of its administration to work-based pension funds and this was retained under each subsequent regime.[120] After 1945 the Manpower division of the British government urged the imposition of a state-administered form of flat-rate payment provision based on the recommendations of the Beveridge report.[121] This was supported by all the occupying powers but opposed by the insurance companies, the medical profession, Handwerk and the trade

---

117. See Egon Tuchtfeld, 'Handwerk' in *Staatslexikon: Rechtswissenschaft - Gesellschaft*, Freiburg 1986, Vol. 2, pp. 1201–13.
118. See chapter one, pp. 5–19.
119. See chapter two, pp. 34–43.
120. See Tampke, 'Bismarck's Social Legislation'.
121. W. Beveridge, *Social Insurance and Allied Benefits*, London 1942.

unions.[122] The first priority of the British, however, was the swiftest possible implementation of a social security system financed from the contributions of the local population and no reform was made.[123]

During the first Christian Democratic-led Parliament of 1949–53, the Bismarckian system was reinstated with the support of the SPD and the trade unions.[124] Adenauer established a special commission in order to provide a comprehensive reorganization of the social security system which was published in 1955 and became known as the Rothenfels Memorandum.[125] The report argued that companies generate costs which are externalized through the provision of public goods such as education, welfare, housing and transport. It recommended targeting companies for an appropriate contribution to social provision. This was to be achieved by organizing employers into federations which would be responsible for compensating for loss of income in case of accident, illness, rehabilitation and seasonal unemployment. Hockerts writes that according to the Rothenfels Memorandum, 'not only were the employers to be responsible for direct labour costs, but for most of the reproduction costs of labour as well'.[126]

Drawing upon the subsidiarity principle, the report argued for the use of organizations which mediate between the individual and the market, such as Handwerk, the trade unions and the firm, as a means of administering welfare and organizing insurance. It was the responsibility of the state to both guarantee subsistence and create the conditions in which smaller organizations could fulfil their function effectively. It was in this context that the work of Alexander Rüstow was drawn upon through the idea of equality of opportunity conceived in terms of the distribution of starting points from which people engage in social activity.[127] The report also recommended the 'right to work' and

122. Hockerts argues that it was the representation from the ADGB in the British zone that was decisive. See Hockerts, pp. 317–22.
123. The Sterling convertibility crisis in 1947 precluded delay.
124. Hockerts, p. 321.
125. Hockerts, p. 326.
126. Hockerts, p. 327.
127. See chapter two, pp. 50–5.

stressed the role that social benefits played as a 'precondition for the productive employment of resources'.[128]

This provided the basis of the pension reform of 1957 in which the level of payment was raised by 60 per cent. In this reform the gap between the benefits based on previous wage and price levels and the rapid rise in costs was bridged by the creation of 'dynamic' pensions (*Dynamische Rente*). This was achieved by not assessing contributions at the rate at which they were paid but converting them into the value of current wage levels and adjusting the pension payment accordingly. The differential between the earnings of those presently working and those who had retired was thus narrowed.[129] The pension of the insured person increased if the average wage of the employed person rose and was set at 60 per cent of earnings.[130] There has been a 617 per cent increase in pension levels between 1957 and 1989 while prices have only risen by 187 per cent. The relative increases have been largest for the manual worker whose pension level has increased by 855 per cent since 1957.[131]

By 1989 there were 33 million people insured by the statutory retirement pension scheme. The link between pensions and the level of earnings also meant that differentials would be maintained in retirement. The pension scheme is thus based on the preservation of relative social status. The administration of pensions is run by self-governing institutions and controlled by parity representation between employers and employees.[132] The incentive to pursue

---

128. The extent to which the subsidiarity principle organized Christian Democratic thinking on social insurance is indicated by the Child Allowance Bill of 1954 in which responsibility was transferred to the employers. Hockerts, pp. 327–8.

129. See Hockerts, p. 321.

130. This was amended in 1984 so that after forty-five years of contributions an insured person on an average wage would receive 70 per cent of average net earnings of all insured persons. Smith, pp. 207–8.

131. Smith, pp. 209–11.

132. Smith, p. 206. The pension scheme is administered by eighteen regional insurance funds. Each fund is an independent self-governing organization. The executive committee is composed of equal numbers of elected representatives of trade unions and employers' associations, elected every six years. As pensions constituted 29.4 per cent of the 'Social' budget of the FRG in 1990, the degree of transfer payments remains considerable. Employers and employees contribute 64.9 per cent of social insurance, the three levels of government contribute the remainder.

short-term advantage is thus constrained by mutual dependence on the long-term performance of the sector and the firm. Through this means society insures itself, status is maintained and redistribution effected.

Currency Reform and Industrial Growth

It has been argued in this chapter that through the establishment of institutions of 'national skill formation', German society was restored. This argument contradicts the exaggerated role given to currency reforms in creating the conditions for economic growth.[133] The IMF played no role as convertibility was not attained until 1958. A substantive state policy towards industry, which included direct investment, tax breaks and the restoration of work organizations, offset the poor investment results that resulted from Erhard's currency reforms.[134]

Abelshauser argues that:

> The heroic legend of German reconstruction as a spontaneous upsurge of aggressive private enterprise is indeed without foundation. In the beginning of the 'Wirtschaftswunder' there was much more planning, state intervention and direct control than could be compatible with *any* concept of a full market economy . . . The heart of any capitalist system, capital formation, was not integrated into the market economy at all.[135]

The structural adjustment required by Erhard's fiscal policy, however, 'had disastrous consequences for the distribution of real incomes and wealth' by 'shifting the burden of tax from property and profits to lower income groups'.[136] Its costs were 'born exclusively by propertyless wage earners – whose savings would have

---

133. For the use of 'myth' in describing the status of currency reform see Abelshauser, 'Economic Policy of Ludwig Erhard', p. 7. Also see Tribe, pp. 203–40. Wolf, p. 32

134. Abelshauser, 'Economic Policy of Ludwig Erhard', p. 11. Emphasis in the original.

135. Ibid., p. 21.

136. Ibid., pp. 9–10. Carlin, p. 39. See also W.W. Heller, 'The Role of Fiscal Monetary Policy in the German Economic Recovery', *American Economic Review*, Vol. 40, No. 2, 1950, pp. 543–6. Heller argues that half the unemployment of 9.3 per cent in 1949 was caused by deflationary polices.

been wiped out by the currency reform, who owned no shares, housing or property and who had no collateral with which they might soften the impact of adjustment'.[137]

The currency reforms led to a decline in the value of savings which was combined with a high increase in progressive tax rates. Wolf argues that the tax returns saved the reforms as they financed direct state investment in industry. The 1952 Investments Assistance Act gave tax breaks to those investing in the large production-based industries.[138] A range of policies were also introduced by the post-war government to distribute the burdens of adjustment more equitably.[139] It is not the recovery of German industry between 1947 and 1953, however, that requires explanation. There was vast excess capacity in the economy and Germany started from a lower productive base than other economies due to the breakdown of the transport system in 1945.[140] Holger Wolf argues that:

> If there is indeed a miracle to be found in West Germany's post-war performance it must thus be looked for in the second stage, the continued expansion of productive capabilities after the re-attainment of capacity output.[141]

It has been argued that this second wave between 1953 and 1961, in which production was twice the 1938 level, was due to the democratic organization of industrial relations, the preservation and integration of craft and mechanical skills within the economic system, and an active state policy of promoting industrial and Handwerk production. Germany was a productive not a financial economy and the strength of its currency was based upon its high value added superiority in the production of consumer goods.[142]

---

137. Tribe, pp. 238–9.

138. Parnell, p. 72. Wolf, pp. 49–53. Carlin, p. 61.

139. See pp. 79–82.

140. Until 1951 Germany's economic growth was below the European average. See Wolf, p. 45, Table 2.11.

141. Wolf, p. 50.

142. Crouch argues that more durable institutional relationships could be forged with the banks than with capital markets and that this enabled German companies to plan further ahead and be more resilient to hostile take-overs. The stock exchange remains weak as a source of venture capital. Crouch, 'Co-operation and Competition', p. 89.

Conclusion

It was argued that the occupying powers in West Germany were distinguished by their internal mode of governance: the United States multi-national capitalist, the British welfare-socialist. Neither succeeded in imposing their welfare or industrial systems on Germany but the difference between them allowed a degree of autonomy within which German society could be restored. In this process the degree of democracy in the economy was expanded, the extent of welfare rights increased and the role of apprenticeship and craft organizations strengthened. The occupying powers should not take too much credit for the rebuilding of German society; they drew the line but did not make the point.[143]

It has also been argued that a strong idea of justice within the firm coupled with the democratic 'negotiation of the burdens' was the foundation of economic success. Co-determination fixed labour as a factor of production and obliged a negotiated strategy in response to external pressures. Handwerk institutions preserved a set of practices and knowledge while administering the vocational training structures. A dense and interconnected network of self-organized institutions preserved the culture of society while securing its protection through the provision of welfare and the preservation of skills.

Catholic and socialist values dominated the political choices available to the West German electorate in 1949.[144] This was expressed in the *Land* Constitution of Hesse, for example, which called for the socialization of basic industries and the rights of workers to participate in the economic management of their companies. This was ratified in a referendum with a large majority in early 1947. Bremen, Württemberg, South Baden and Berlin also passed constitutions calling for the socialization of industry.[145] West

---

143. Lord Kaldor, for example, claimed that the British 'gave' Germany their industrial relations system and argued that Britain should in effect adopt a system it had itself created. See Dartmann, p. 47. Streeck also makes a similar claim in 'Co-determination after Four Decades', p. 140.

144. The trade unions conceived of the new Republic as much as a correction of the defects of Weimar as a continuation of its practices. For an account of the discontinuities with Weimar see Dartmann, pp. 76–8.

145. These were vetoed by the US and France. The British suspended a socialization law in North Rhine Westphalia in August 1948. See Eisenberg, p. 303.

German society was restored after Nazism on the basis of democratic association and individual rights through the re-definition of liberal democracy. It developed a liberal state and a democratically governed economy.

4

Solidarity

Land and Labour in Poland: 1945–1980

Land, labour and the productive organizations of society formed the elements around which political conflict clustered in Poland after 1945.[1] As regards land, by the end of the 1940s, as a result of the break-up of large estates and the expropriation of previously German property, 'approximately ninety-three per cent of all agrarian land in Poland was owned by the farmers who worked it'.[2] Private landownership expanded under Communist rule leading to an enlarged small-holding peasantry.[3] A policy of collectivization was initiated in the early 1950s but by the end of 1956, following riots in Poznan in which seventy-two people were killed, the collective farms were effectively disbanded.[4] The United Peasants' Party were represented in the institutions of state through their permanent membership of the ruling coalition. Price subsidies and guaranteed grain quotas remained until 1989.

As regards labour, until the mid 1960s Polish workers enjoyed

---

1. In 1956 (Ochab), 1970 (Gomulka), 1980 (Gierek) and 1981 (Kania), a change of leadership and policy resulted from labour protests.

2. Krystina Daniel, 'Private Ownership in a Changing Poland: Myth and Reality' in G. S. Alexander and G. Skapska, eds, *A Fourth Way? Privatisation, Property and the Emergence of New Market Economies*, London 1994, pp. 138–49, p. 138.

3. Thirty per cent of privately cultivated land derived from reforms initiated after 1945, *ibid.*, p. 139. In 1989 there were 2.7 million private farms in Poland with an average size of 7.2 hectares.

4. The number of collective farms fell from 10,150 on 30 September to 1,534 on 31 December 1956. See Michael H. Bernhard, *The Origins of Democratization in Poland: Workers, Intellectuals and Oppositional Politics, 1976–1980*, New York 1993, p. 34.

uninterrupted economic growth, negligible unemployment and an improvement in their living standards.[5] Housing, basic foodstuffs, education and health care were provided either free of charge or with substantial subsidies.[6] There were significant improvements in literacy, nutrition and life expectancy. The deal imposed by the PZPR (Polish United Workers' Party) after 1948 was that basic political liberties would be surrendered in return for guaranteed subsistence.[7] Many were cold but few were frozen. As with the Speenhamland system in England and the Bismarckian welfare state, the provision of welfare was combined with the banning of independent trade unions. While workers had a 'degree of shop-floor power independent of any formal union organisation', they did not enjoy the right to associate legally or to negotiate independently of party mediation.[8] There were no public procedures of conflict resolution.

The relations of production were set in 1947 when a strike of textile workers in Lodz was broken by the police and army.[9] Following the riots of 1956, however, Gomulka came to power and his programme of economic reforms included the revival of works councils as well as the privatization of agriculture. While the latter was granted, in 1957 a strike by transport workers in Lodz was broken militarily. An Act was passed in 1958 which removed the right to works councils from the constitution.[10]

On 12 December 1970 the announcement of a 30 per cent rise in food prices was the trigger for sit-down strikes in the shipyards

5. For an analysis of the growth rates in industrial production, investment and real incomes see Ivan Mazor, 'The Decay of the Command Economies,' *East-European Economy and Society*, Vol. 8, No. 2, 1994.

6. See Oliver MacDonald, 'The Polish Vortex: Solidarity and Socialism', *New Left Review*, No. 139, 1983, pp. 5–48.

7. See Ray Taras, *Ideology in a Socialist State: Poland 1956–1983*, Cambridge 1984, p. 48.

8. Charles F. Sabel and David Stark, 'Planning, Politics and Shop-Floor Power: Hidden Forms of Bargaining in Soviet-Imposed State-Socialist Societies', *Politics and Society*, Vol. 11, No. 4, 1982, 439–75, p. 449.

9. In 1951 a sit-down strike in the Dabrowa basin was similarly resolved. See Jaime Reynolds, 'Communists, Socialists and Workers: Poland 1944–1948', *Soviet Studies*, Vol. 30, No. 4, 1978, pp. 516–39.

10. See January Kostrewski, 'Na smierc rad rebotniczych,' *Biuletyn Informacyjny* 26, 1978, pp. 16–20. See also Daniel Singer, *The Road To Gdansk*, London 1982, pp. 251–3.

of the Baltic coast.[11] Their first demand was that 'trade unions be freed from control or interference by the PZPR and the workplace management'.[12] The formation of independent trade unions brought Solidarity into collision with the managerial claims of the Leninist state.[13] Four workers were shot dead in Gdansk on 15 December and four more followed in Gdynia two days later. A general strike was called in Szczecin during which an interfactory strike committee presented their proposals for reform. These included the establishment of an independent union and the abolition of the nomenklatura system.[14] After three days two workers were killed. On 20 December Gierek replaced Gomulka on a platform of economic reform based upon a greater integration of the works councils in the management of the firm.[15] Food prices were frozen at their 1966 levels, seven billion zlotys were allocated to low income workers and a crash housing programme was initiated.[16] Another aspect of the reforms was that 164 of the largest industrial enterprises were placed under the direct supervision of the central committee.[17] Simultaneously Gierek turned to the West for massive loans. By 1976, 43 per cent of all plant technology was less than five years old.[18]

Far from modernizing production, however, Western investment was based on exporting obsolete technology.[19] There was no

---

11. Shipbuilding was Poland's primary customized export. In 1970, Poland occupied tenth place in tonnage of ships produced and was fifth in the foreign sales of ships. Roman Laba, *The Roots of Solidarity: A Political Sociology of Poland's Working Class Democratization*, Princeton 1991 (hereafter Laba), p. 121.

12. Laba, p. 45.

13. For an analysis of soviet-style management see Mark Beissinger, *Scientific Management, Socialist Discipline and Soviet Power*, Cambridge Mass. 1988. Sabel and Stark define Leninism as an ideology characterized by the 'centralization of economic control in the hands of self-proclaimed custodians of a higher rationality', p. 446.

14. Laba, pp. 157.

15. See Z.A. Pelcynski, 'The Downfall of Gomulka', in Adam Bromke and John W. Strong, eds, *Gierek's Poland*, New York 1973, pp. 1–23.

16. See Peter Green, 'The Third Round in Poland', *New Left Review*, No. 101–2, 1977, pp. 69–108, p. 71.

17. MacDonald, 'Vortex', p. 11.

18. Green, 'Third Round', p. 79.

19. See Jacek Tittenbrun, *The Collapse of 'Real Socialism' in Poland*, London 1993 (hereafter Tittenbrun), p. 19. Also Zbigniew Fellanbuchl, 'The Polish Economy in the 1970s', *East European Economies Post-Helsinki*, Washington DC, 1977, pp. 832–4. Leszek Balcerowicz, *Socialism, Capitalism and Transformation*, Budapest 1995 (hereafter Balcerowicz), p. 291.

high value added dimension to Polish production; raw materials, agriculture and ship-building remained the mainstays of exports.[20] There was thus an increase in debt without a corresponding improvement in productivity.[21] By 1980 the interest on the $24.1 billion debt exceeded the value of exports, was larger than investment expenditure in the public sector and ten times higher than outlays in industry and agriculture.[22] In short, Poland's debt to Western states and commercial banks increased 23.5 fold between 1970 and 1979 while its productive capacity declined.[23] By 1980 Poland was the third largest debtor in the world.[24]

Repayment was attempted by raising prices, cutting welfare and reducing labour costs. There was an increasing use of piece rates and overtime. Through this means, production bottlenecks, which were frequent due to shortages of imported components, inefficient transport and communications systems as well as strikes, led to no payment of wages.[25] Safety at work was neglected and spending on health, housing and education significantly reduced.[26] In 1976 a one-day strike was called in response to the announcement of a 60 per cent increase in meat prices. In Radom twelve workers were shot dead and 2,000 people arrested.[27] The increase was withdrawn but there was a steady rise in the cost of

20. Raw materials and food products constituted 76 per cent of hard currency exports in 1976. Tittenbrun, p. 19.

21. The state predicted a 20 per cent increase in exports between 1971 and 1973, a 35 per cent surge in 1974 and a sustained increase of 40 per cent from 1975 on. See Joan Zoeter, 'Eastern Europe: The Hard Currency Debt', *East European Economic Assessment*, Washington DC, 1981.

22. Ian Shapiro, 'The Fiscal Crisis of the Polish State: Genesis of the 1980 Strikes', *Theory and Society*, Vol. 10, No. 4, 1981, pp. 469–502.

23. Tittenbrun, p. 13.

24. Tittenbrun, p. 65.

25. The amount of overtime far exceeded the maximum working day stipulated in pre-war labour legislation. Between 1978 and 1979, miners worked on forty-two Sundays, as well as each Saturday, on eleven hour shifts. See George Feiwel, 'Pressures, Breakdown and Optimism in Planning' in *Industrialisation and Planning Under Polish Socialism*, New York 1971, pp. 261–78, See also Tittenbrun, pp. 17–19.

26. The number of occupational diseases per 100,000 employees increased from 51.7 per cent in 1971 to 66.8 in 1980. Between 1972 and 1981 the number of accidents at work increased by 29 per cent and mortal accidents by 14 per cent. While between 1961 and 1965 the size of the social budget was 28.6 per cent of total outlay, between 1971 and 1975 it was 19.3 per cent. Tittenbrun, pp. 26–43.

27. See Michael Bernhard, 'The Strikes of June 1976 in Poland', *East European Politics and Societies*, Vol. 1, No. 3, 1987, pp. 363–92.

living throughout the decade combined with an accumulated drop in real wages.[28] The central committee was under pressure from both creditors and consumers and on 1 July 1980, after a three and a half year gap, the price rises were reinstated.[29]

The reaction was a wave of strikes that continued in various parts of the country for forty-five days. On 14 August the Lenin shipyard in Gdansk initiated a sit-down strike.[30] Gdynia struck the following day and Szczecin followed two days later. A twenty-one point programme written by the interfactory strike committee was presented and the Gdansk Accord between the government and Solidarity was signed on 31 August. This recognized the right to a legal independent union, the representation of works councils in the management of enterprises and the decentralization of economic governance.

By 1981 Solidarity had almost ten million members out of an active working population of seventeen million. It was within the framework of increasing wage differentials, a reduction in welfare and an increase in shift hours combined with an intensification of economic crisis that, over a year after the signing of the Gdansk Accord, Solidarity developed its 'Programme for National Revival'.[31]

Justice and Solidarity: the Principles of Reform

Justice as fairness

The political principles of reform articulated by Solidarity were the constitutional priority of basic human and civil rights of association, conscience and expression.

---

28. See Henryk Flakierski, 'The Polish Economic Reforms' in Simon McInness ed., *The Soviet Union and East Europe into the 1980s*, Ontario 1976, pp. 175–203.

29. For the influence of Western banks on the decision to raise prices see Juan Cameron, 'What the Bankers Did to Poland', *Fortune*, 22 September 1980. Cameron argued that the credit owed to them allowed Western banks to be the 'financial policeman of Poland's government'. *Fortune*, 20 August 1980.

30. For transcripts of the interfactory strike committee proceedings in Gdansk see *Labour Focus*, Vol. 4, No. 1–3.

31. Solidarity, 'Programme Adopted by the First National Congress', in Peter Raina, ed., *Poland 1981: Towards Social Renewal*, London 1981, pp. 326–90 (hereafter Solidarity). This was compiled from the motions submitted to their first Congress which took place in two stages between 5–10 September and 26 September–7 October 1981. Some 896 delegates representing 9.5 million members were present.

The system must guarantee basic civil freedoms and respect the principles of equality before the law as far as all citizens and all public institutions are concerned . . . regardless of their convictions, political views and organizational affiliations.[32]

A partisan state based on a single party with institutionalized privileges for its members contradicted Solidarity's definition of citizenship which was consistent with that developed by John Rawls in *A Theory of Justice*.[33] This rests on the premise that fairness is the fundamental value of modern political societies and provides the foundation for three principles which serve as ground rules for regulating the terms of social co-operation.[34] The first principle states that each person has an equal right to a full scheme of liberties compatible with an identical right for all. The second is that of equal opportunity and the third is the 'difference principle' which proposes that inequality is justified as long as the welfare of the least advantaged is not diminished.[35] This is expressed in thesis 4 of the Solidarity document which states that economic reform 'should be in line with the principle of protecting the weakest groups of the population'.[36] The price to be paid for economic reform, Solidarity argued, was the amount of inequality necessary to improve the conditions of the most disadvantaged:

> In its policy the union will be governed by the principle that the terms of transition must guarantee the real income level of the less prosperous part of society. While acting with equal concern for each citizen we will accord particular solicitude to the poorest.[37]

---

32. Solidarity, p. 349. Also see pp. 330, 327, 351.

33. Solidarity, p. 381. Data on the attitudes of Polish workers to their working conditions and political treatment indicate widespread sentiments of injustice. In the study commissioned by the central committee of the PZPR of workers' demands in 2,800 large factories throughout Poland, freedom of speech and equal access to educational institutions were ranked highest. More than 50 per cent considered that they were being exploited. See Bernhard, *The Origins of Democratization*, p. 68.

34. See John Rawls, 'The Basic Liberties and their Priority', in *The Tanner Lectures on Human Values*, Vol. 3, Cambridge 1982.

35. Rawls, TOJ, pp. 258–319, 90–5.

36. Solidarity, thesis 4, p. 334. For other expressions of this principle in the 1981 document see pp. 336, 378, which proposes 'the principle of protecting absolutely the weakest groups in the population'.

37. Solidarity, p. 334.

Solidarity defined a good society as one which provided the 'conditions of a life free of poverty, exploitation, fear and deception, in a society that is democratically and lawfully organised'.[38] If reforms disregard the distribution of the material conditions necessary for effective association, a large number of citizens may be excluded from the benefits of public activity. The satisfaction of needs is as important as procedural justice.[39] This justifies the provision of what Rawls calls 'primary goods', defined as those things necessary for social agency.[40] Rawls's solution to the existence of formal equality and substantive inequality is to justify the tax levels necessary to redistribute those goods without which agency would be impossible. Welfare is thus conceived by Rawls as a precondition of individual liberty. While Rawls wishes to achieve this through redistributive taxation, Solidarity placed a greater emphasis on the equitable distribution of power within the economy. Individual rights, state impartiality and the priority of the poorest defined the theory of justice developed by Solidarity.[41]

Enterprise democracy

The recognition of status, the application of subsidiarity and the establishment of enterprise democracy formed the basis of the programme of economic reforms proposed by Solidarity in 1981. They analysed three related deficiencies in the command economy: centralization, monopoly and arbitrary management. Centralization meant that calculations and forecasts were made on the basis of evidence that was unreliable due to the sheer volume of data, setting aside the veracity of the information received. Party control over the allocation of funds, the appointment of managers and the setting of production goals led to an inefficient distribution of information, the inappropriate promotion of personnel and the exclusion of employees from participation in the management of

---

38. Solidarity, p. 331.

39. This is brought out repeatedly in the Solidarity programme, see particularly p. 355, 343.

40. The list of primary goods is a) the basic rights and liberties, b) freedom of movement and occupation, c) access to positions of responsibility in the political and economic institutions of society and d) income and wealth. Rawls, *Political Liberalism*, p. 181.

41. Solidarity, p. 378.

the enterprise.[42] Initiative was subordinated to directives within a career structure which rewarded conformity.[43] The monopoly of societal resources controlled by the party was to be replaced by the dual strategy of selling stock and the election of management within the enterprise.

The critique of managerial prerogative is developed in thesis 20 of the Solidarity programme:

> A system that combines political and economic power and is based on unceasing interference by party elements in the functioning of enterprises is the main reason for our economy's crisis and for the absence of equal opportunities in vocational and professional life. The party's power of appointment makes impossible any kind of rational personnel policy and turns millions of non-party people into second-class employees. Today the only way to change this situation is to create genuine self-management groups, which would make the workforce true masters of enterprises.[44]

As regards the democratic decentralization and decartelization of the economy, Solidarity wrote that 'the organisational structure of the economy serving the command system must be smashed'.[45] In an exact parallel with the language of the striking miners in the Ruhr in 1917, the miners in the Jastrzebie colliery called for 'decent human treatment' in their working lives.[46] The establishment of 'employees councils' was a means by which the responsibility for decision-making and the knowledge for successful enterprise adaptation were facilitated by access to information and the negotiation of strategic choices by all employees in the firm.[47] Democratic management and the equalization of burdens

42. In September 1981 a survey of workers in two Lodz factories was conducted. The main demand was for a redistribution of power in the firm and constraints on managerial prerogative. See S. Dziecielska-Machnikowska and G. Matuszak, *Czternascie lodzkich miesiecy*, Lodz 1984, p. 187.

43. As a result of Solidarity's victory in 1980, hundreds of sets of demands written by workers in 1970, 1971 and 1980 were deposited in the Gdansk Archive. Laba's analysis of the strike documents reveals a concern, above all, with the inefficiency of cadre selection. pp. 155–66.

44. Solidarity, p. 346.

45. Solidarity, p. 330.

46. T. Matysiak, *Przed Konfliktem - Konflikt*, Warsaw 1986, p. 54.

47. Elections were to take place biennially and individual representatives could serve for no longer than two terms. Solidarity, p. 397.

within the enterprise were the basis of societal restoration and economic reform.

> It is possible to overcome our crisis because, by implementing a comprehensive and profound reform, we shall be able to tap all those reserves of industriousness and enterprise rooted in our society that have not been tapped so far.[48]

Solidarity analysed the principal reason for industrial decline and the debt crisis as despotic management.[49] Recognizing the severity of the crisis, they argued that enterprise democracy would serve as a form of wage substitution during the recession that would necessarily ensue. Authoritarian management, Solidarity argued, disregarded the needs of the enterprise and the status of the employee.[50] In what reads like a summary of Karl Polanyi's central thesis in *The Great Transformation*, they wrote:

> Work is for man, and what determines its sense is its closeness to man, to his real needs. Our national and social rebirth must be based on the restored hierarchy of those goals. While defining its aims, Solidarity draws from the values of Christian ethics, from our national traditions and from the workers' and democratic traditions of the labour world.[51]

The State Enterprise and Employee Self-Management Acts were passed by the Sejm in October 1981. The latter ensured that works councils played a central role in the appointment of managers and the development of enterprise strategy.[52] The State Enterprise Act forbade the direct state interference in the management of the firm

---

48. Solidarity, p. 367.

49. In the Bielsko-Biala region 120 factories were shut for ten days in 1980 by workers demanding a change in management. Other corruption strikes occurred throughout the Baltic region. See C. Harman, *Class Struggles in Eastern Europe 1945–1983*, London 1988, p. 265.

50. Solidarity, p. 326. The poor quality of management was a constant source of dissatisfaction and provided the pragmatic rationale of the demand for enterprise democracy. Laba, p. 122.

51. Solidarity, p. 327. In this thesis Solidarity refer to the encyclical *Laborem Exercens* as an ideological resource. Written by John-Paul II, this called for the 'co-ownership of the means of production' and defends the status of labour as the 'primary cause' in economic activity. See chapter two, pp. 34–43.

52. Some 400 firms, however, retained centralized appointment practices due to their 'special importance to the state'. See S. Ryszard Domanski, 'The Quest for Ownership: A response to the "surprise literature"', *Eastern European Economics*, Vol. 32, No. 2, 1994, pp. 71–94, p. 81.

and allowed enterprises to issue bonds and shares.[53] Privatization would take place through the co-determination of the enterprise. Owners and labour would be represented on the supervisory board in each privatized company.[54] Solidarity, as was the case with the ADGB in West Germany after 1945, made all other goals subordinate to co-determination, threatening a general strike if it were not implemented.[55] An 'unfettered' economic democracy, not a free labour market, was Solidarity's main policy objective.[56]

The self-governing republic

The self-governing republic (*Samorzadna Rzeczpospolita*) established three distinct spheres of societal organization. The first concerned the establishment of a legal state based on the priority of individual human rights. The second was the self-governed enterprise as the primary economic unit. The third was subsidiarity, defined as the greatest degree of decentralization in democratic decision-making. The construction of a legitimate state required a substantive society to represent.

The reform of the state institutions in Poland had to obey two potentially conflicting principles, those of liberalism and democracy. A liberal democracy is a potentially incoherent amalgam since the priority of individual rights limits democratic authority while majoritarian domination is a threat to liberty.[57] Solidarity confronted this problem by combining the priority of rights with the extension of municipal and sectoral democracy.[58] They proposed a 'systems democracy' in which the legal, medical and educational sectors would each run their own affairs without direct state interference by means of self-governing professional associations.[59] This, they argued, would raise 'professional ethics' and

---

53. Balcerowicz, p. 275.

54. Poland adopted the two-tier board structure practised in Germany.

55. Solidarity also called, as did the ADGB, for the labour director within the enterprise to be elected directly by the employees, p. 338.

56, Solidarity, p. 395.

57. See chapter one, pp. 3–5.

58. Solidarity, p. 348.

59. For the outline of these self-governing measures in the legal, medical, scientific and educational systems, see thesis, 24, pp. 350, 345; thesis 30, p. 355; and thesis 29, p. 354.

'restore proper status' within scientific, academic and professional organizations.[60]

> The formation of organizations independent of the state authorities is to be regarded as a fact fundamental for changes taking place in our country's socio-political relations. Owing to them, society is able to strive to realize its aspirations and effectively defend its rights.[61]

The intermediate institutions envisaged by Solidarity were a precondition for sustaining the conditions of justice.[62] Solidarity had learnt from 1970, 1976 and 1980 that without recognized and democratic social agents, a legal order can be easily overturned in times of crisis.[63]

The spectre haunting communism in Poland was the democratically organized labour movement and its commitment to civil liberties in politics and democratic power in the economy. In Poland in 1981, as in France in 1848, the army was sent in to arrest the leaders, its organizations were outlawed, illegality was praised in the name of market reforms, and democracy in the economy was decried as damaging to the national interest. The nomination of management by the state was restored during martial law by expanding the list of the 400 companies excluded from the 1981 Acts.[64] The imposition of martial law did not succeed, however, in extirpating the ghost of Solidarity. Although ten thousand union activists were imprisoned, the decentralized structure of the union was flexible enough to mount rolling strikes which in May 1988 forced the party to share power. Laba is correct to argue that Solidarity was 'the first working class movement to play a leading theoretical and practical role in the removal of a regime from office.'[65]

After 1989, however, a policy of state centralization in the name

---

60. Solidarity, pp. 345, 355.
61. Solidarity, pp. 328, 386.
62. Solidarity, p. 346. See chapter one, pp. 5–19.
63. Durkheim argued that the constraints enforced by autonomous societal organizations serve as a 'framework' for individuals and a 'skeleton' for society. Without them, he argued, a society 'becomes so unstable as to be liable to disintegration if it suffers the least shock'. Emile Durkheim, *Professional Ethics and Civic Morals*, London 1992, p. 106.
64. See Domanski, p. 82.
65. Laba, p. 182. See also Tittenbrun, pp. 255–7.

of creating competition was re-enacted, the self-governing republic was discarded and enterprise democracy abolished. The industrial economy collapsed and with it the state budget. Solidarity subsequently dissolved into the state in the name of market reforms and within five years the former Communist Party was elected to office in order to continue the policies they had initiated in 1981. The next chapter is an analysis of the changes in the inernational consensus which facilitated this development.

5

The Rise of the
New Right

This chapter is an analysis of the reasons for the ascendancy of the New Right in the 1980s. This effected a change in the consensus which transformed the terms of political rationality. The US, UK, NATO, the World Bank and IMF retained their previously dominant position, but the ideological justification of their continued hegemony was redefined. In order to understand the transformation in Poland, it is necessary to analyse how significant changes in a political consensus alter the agenda, defined as the feasible scope of policy, by redefining the practical possibilities for rational and credible action.

The Crisis of the Post-War Settlement

The three nations which exercised the greatest influence in the construction of the post-war European settlement experienced what was widely perceived as a 'crisis' during the 1970s. In economic terms Britain and the United States experienced an increase in unemployment and a declining share of the world market. It was during this period that any notion of economic and technological parity with the West was dropped by the Soviet Union.

The definition of a crisis adopted here is that an existing arrangement is perceived to be unstable and incapable of sustaining itself without radical change. Secondly, it is a phenomenon of limited duration. Either the regime collapses due to the correctly defined instability, or it survives, thus falsifying the analysis. Permanent crisis, like permanent revolution, is a conceptual and historical fallacy. Finally, a crisis is also a period in which previously unconsidered or discredited options and experiences are re-evaluated as legitimate resources out of which reconstruction and resolution can be fashioned. Rationality is redefined as part of any resolution of a significant crisis.

The crisis in Britain and the US was interpreted as involving the internal and external erosion of liberty and authority in both state and market. The adoption of a radical programme designed to sustain the dominant agents of the post-war settlement, and the successful mobilization of political forces to implement this, was most successful in these two countries. No other major industrial powers implemented the measures proposed by what came to be known as the 'New Right'. The election of Margaret Thatcher as British Prime Minister in 1979 was of crucial significance in its international success. This was not merely the replacement of one administration by another but was the political equivalent of what Kuhn calls a paradigm shift.[1]

The New Right

National agenda

The internal agenda of the New Right can be summarized in the following way. There was a redistribution of wealth and power from poor to rich through the cumulative cutting of taxation on high earners and the curtailment of welfare rights. Corporate taxes were eased, while the responsibilities of the state shifted from extending citizenship rights to providing subsistence. This was justified through the use of an economic model in which the increasing bureaucratization and stagnation of the economy was to be reversed by the unleashing of entrepreneurial forces provoked by tax cuts. The effects of incentive-driven innovation were argued to be beneficial for all in aggregate terms as overall economic growth and fiscal stability would be to the general benefit. Greater inequality did not necessarily decrease the welfare of the poorest if there was overall pie growth.

The elimination of labour organizations from influence on government through either formal or informal arrangements

---

1. Thomas S. Kuhn, *The Structure of Scientific Revolutions*, 2nd edn, Chicago 1970.

follows from this. The abolition of restrictive practices in employment and production was considered to be necessary and good. The 'free market' was a means of institutionalizing a model in which economic solidarity was seen as irrational while enforcing discipline at the firm level through a re-assertion of management's right to manage. Labour was restored to its commodity form. The post-war strategy of working-class co-option was replaced by exclusion in the name of justice and the individual was conceived as sovereign in both state and economy as citizen and consumer respectively.[2] Institutionalized trade union power was seen as both anti-democratic and economically damaging. The idea of structuring markets through democratic organization was rejected as unfeasible and immoral. State intervention created structurally imposed disequilibrium and the elimination of freedom defined as uncoerced co-operation by means of voluntary contract.[3] The labour market had to be liberated from the 'feudal' privileges bestowed upon unions during the post-war settlement.[4]

Public ownership was viewed as a relic of the war economy in times of peace. Nationalization was an archaic expression of an erroneous ideology and had been superseded by a new system of international competition. A national industrial policy was seen as a delusion, although the importance of a national monetary policy became an increasingly important responsibility of government. The principal argument of the New Right was that the state could not co-ordinate the information necessary to successfully plan or run an economy in which decentralized decision-making by necessarily ignorant agents was the only means of distributing information.[5] Market economies were beyond the conscious design of any single agency, even one as powerful as the state. The globalization of trade rendered state calculated macro-economic

---

2. For an analysis of the post-war settlement see Samuel Bowles, David Gordon and Thomas Weisskopf, 'Power, Accumulation and Crisis: The Rise and Demise of the Post-war Social Structure of Accumulation', in Samuel Bowles and Richard Edwards, eds, *Radical Political Economy*, Vol. 2, Aldershot 1990.

3. For a review of the New Right analysis of the post-war settlement see Richard Lockett, *Thinking the Unthinkable*, London 1994.

4. For the description of trade unions as feudal institutions and the 'chief source of Britain's economic decline', see F.A. Hayek, *Economic Freedom*, London 1972, p. 321.

5. See chapter one.

planning an anachronism, its pursuit the result of intellectual error and demagogic politics.[6]

The police and army, however, were increased in size and resources and remained the exclusive responsibility of the state. US military spending was an important motor for implicit Keynesian state-sponsored reflation in the 1980s and no privatization was considered in this sphere.[7] Autonomous organizations with their own mode of governance yet dependent on the state for resources, public corporations, were subject to political pressure to conform to market demands.

The New Right agenda can be summarized in the following way. The state had no direct role as a producer and state-owned assets were to be liquidated and sold as privately owned public companies. The status of consumer was to subordinate that of citizen in their conception of public service. The state's role as provider was to be strictly limited in that the market was seen as the principle means of resource exchange and allocation. The welfare state ceased to be the means of extending citizenship but a necessary mechanism for ameliorating poverty. Monopoly state printing rights as regards currency assumed a primary position in the development of macro-economic policy. Productivity, employment and distributional equity were subordinated to the demands of a sound currency and financial discipline. The Treasury was reaffirmed as the principle economic ministry and industrial policy was abandoned. Its role as policeman was increased and reinvigorated through a material increase in resources, status and wage levels. New public order laws were passed where the existing ones were considered inadequate. The role as internal policeman was matched by an increase in the size and technological capacity of the army, and as the US and British armies were to play the role of 'global policeman' in the New World Order it is appropriate to examine the international dimensions of the New Right agenda.

International agenda

The international agenda ran parallel to the domestic one. There was an international transfer of wealth from poor to rich and an

---

6. Hayek, *Errors*.
7. For the scale of US military Keynesianism see Arrighi, pp. 320–4.

increasing use of proxy armies against regimes which resisted the commodification of labour and land.[8] The three principle organizations responsible for the reproduction and enforcement of the new political, military and economic regime were increased in size and power. NATO, the World Bank and the IMF were all given an enhanced role.[9] The deregulation of financial markets gave the impression of a strengthening of the economies in both the US and Britain as the increase in the money flowing through the national economies provoked a consumer and property boom in international centres of financial trading such as New York and London. If military and financial transactions are discounted, however, there was an intensification of manufacturing decline in both countries throughout the 1980s.[10]

The failure of the Mitterrand experiment

The failure of the Mitterrand 'experiment' between 1981 and 1983 became a central justification for the rationality of New Right policies. Evidence that such an experiment was undertaken, let alone failed, is difficult to find.[11] The policy of worker self-management was not implemented.[12] Its income policy was constrained by financial prudence and the expansion of welfare limited.[13] Only in terms of educational reform could there be said to have been an

---

8. Covert terrorist policies were pursued in Africa (Mozambique), Central America (Nicaragua, El Salvador, Guatemala), South America (Chile, Bolivia, Uruguay), South East Asia (Thailand, Malaysia, Indonesia). For a rational choice approach to the efficiency of using this tactic see T. David Mason and Dale A. Krane, 'The Political-Economy of the Death Squads: Towards a Theory of the Impact of State Sanctioned Terror', *International Studies Quarterly*, Vol. 33, 1989, pp. 199–231.

9. The ILO, WHO and UNICEF were appropriately 'downsized'.

10. See Edgar Wilson, *A Very British Miracle*, London 1992, p. 111.

11. See Marc Lombard, 'A Re-examination of the Reasons for the Failure of Keynesian Expansionary Policies in France, 1981–1983', *Cambridge Journal of Economics*, Vol. 19, 1995, pp. 359–72 (hereafter Lombard).

12. See Daniel Singer, *Is Socialism Doomed?*, Oxford 1991, pp. 13–56. The nationalization policy raised the share of state-owned companies from 5 to 8 per cent of GDP between 1981 and 1983, but this was scarcely drastic and was justified as a rationalization measure.

13. There was an increase in the minimum wage of 10.6 per cent between June 1981 and December 1982. This was combined with an hourly rate increase of 5.3 per cent over the same period and a one-hour reduction in the working week. Due to this, disposable incomes rose by 6.5 per cent. Fiscal policy, however, was far from experimental, although the level of VAT was increased in luxury goods and

experimental policy, though increases in expenditure were not particularly significant.[14] The Mauroy government attempted to introduce some restrictions on international capital mobility and currency control but abandoned them swiftly as the value of the franc fell by 20 per cent between 1981 and 1983. The time lag necessary to reap the benefit in exports was not permitted to pass before austerity measures and a deflationary policy were introduced.

In his analysis of the causes of Keynesian failure, Jeffrey Sachs argued that the increase in real unit labour costs brought about by the increase in the minimum wage and holidays combined with the reduction in working hours, led to a severance of price and value as these policies worsened France's comparative trading position.[15] The increased welfare spending and redistributionary measures exacerbated this. The wage gap, however, increased only fractionally between 1980 and 1981 and improved thereafter.[16] Lombard argues that 'the sheer timidity of the expansion led to the failure of the experiment'.[17] His reason for arguing this is that the world recession reduced foreign demand for French exports by 5 per cent. Exports accounted for 20 per cent of French GDP before 1982 so the economy contracted by about 1 per cent. The increase in the budget, however, was only 0.4 per cent of GDP and for this reason the expansion was unable to compensate for the contraction in export demand. A significant success of this policy, however, was to slow down the rate of unemployment growth to 1.9 per cent over the two years as compared to a 5 per cent increase in Germany and an 8 per cent increase in Britain.

Ultimately, the consideration given to labour in the policies pursued by the first Mitterrand government was opposed by the resurgent financial community. The modestly expansionary

---

decreased on necessities. Contrary to the prevailing myth there was no large increase in the liquidity ratio (the net supply growth [M2] as a percentage of GDP) which was far less expansionary than under the Giscard government between 1976 and 1979. Interest rates were raised to protect the franc.

14. See George Ross, Stanley Hoffman and Sylvia Malzacher, eds, *The Mitterrand Experiment*, Cambridge 1987.

15. The early years of the Mitterrand presidency provided the first public occasion for Jeffrey Sachs to develop his critique of socialism. See J. Sachs and C. Wyplosz, 'The Economic Consequences of Mitterrand's Economic Policy', in M. Bruno and J. Sachs, eds, *Economics of Worldwide Stagflation*, Cambridge Mass. 1986.

16. Lombard, p. 369.

17. Lombard, p. 369.

policies introduced by Mauroy were undertaken at a time of severe recession and the high point of international market deregulation.[18] The introduction of rent control for private sector housing, marginal tax rate increases and modest nationalization were opposed to the principles of the prevailing regulatory regime in the international political economy. Speculation against the franc was intensified until the policy of expansion was retracted. The only defence against the decimation of the franc was provided by conformity to the European Monetary System guidelines on currency policy which required cuts in welfare and wages. France took shelter behind the irreproachability of the deutschmark. The failure of the Mitterrand 'experiment' became an essentially uncontested concept during the politics of the 1980s. Any policy which disputed the definition of economic well being proposed by international currency markets was associated with this failed experiment and on that basis rejected.

The result was that explicitly Social and Christian Democratic forms of government and policy became implicit aspects of regime organization. They were defended not in terms of their justice and efficiency but as impossible to reform due to political constraints or the burdens of history. State welfare provision, trade union participation, artisan privileges and progressive taxation were not defined as constitutive features of successful societies but as historical anomalies with only contingent value and particular functions. Those aspects of economic and political organizations that conformed to market principles and models of fiscal and managerial control were emphasized. The Deutsche Bank became the trade-mark of German economic success through their commitment to fiscal probity.[19] There was a shift from industry to finance, politics to markets, work to prices, manufacturing to monetary targets. A formal conception of the economy replaced the substantive assumptions that underlay the institutional arrangements characteristic of the post-war settlement.[20]

The political consequence was that the comparative superiority

---

18. See P.A. Muet, 'Economic Management and the International Environment 1981–83', in H. Machin and V. Wright, eds, *Economic and Policy Making Under the Mitterrand Presidency 1981–84*, London 1985.

19. See chapter three, pp. 82–4.

20. See chapter one, pp. 5–19.

of welfare capitalist regimes generally and the social market in particular was not articulated as an ideology with the necessary components of a coherent theory of history, rationality and human nature. The New Right had all three and it is the success of the ideology as an explanation of crisis and a means to its solution, as well as the absence of a counter narrative which could have challenged it effectively, that led to general European acquiescence to American and British ideological domination of the international agenda, and their subsequent control of the key institutions of global economic and military enforcement.

This section has attempted to analyse the meaning of crisis and give a description of the New Right goals and the absence of an alternative. The next section is an analysis of the rationality of this change and how the New Right succeeded in mobilizing democratic support for its principles and policies. In order to do this it is necessary to clarify certain concepts used throughout this chapter.

Agency, Context and Consensus

When we refer to agents, whether these be individual, associative or collective in the form of states, it is assumed that they act in a context constituted by others; they are participants in a dynamic historical process. The second assumption is that these identities act purposefully. An agent is not completely determined by the will of another or by a structure. An actor is not always an agent; their ability to act can be destroyed by superior external might.[21] An agent always has a degree of conscious and recognized autonomy in how they play their part. The Jews and Gypsies of the Nazi-occupied lands in 1943 were not agents, neither was the Lithuanian state during the Soviet invasion of 1941.[22] A prisoner

---

21. This takes the form of imposing limits on communication and self-organization. The identity of Buddhists in Tibet precedes the rule of Communists by many thousand years. The Tibetan Buddhist identity is logically independent of, and temporally prior to, Communism. However, as Buddhists they are denied any means of agency by Communist rule. Buddhists in Tibet are actors but not agents.

22. Some Jews and Gypsies succeeded in escaping from the direct domination of their would-be executioners. Their survival, however, depended on either isolation or the effacement of their communal identity and civil personality.

is not an agent until he has either the capacity to organize escape or the ability to achieve remission through good behaviour.

The third point is that no agent acts in order to create a worse outcome, at least in the long term.[23] Actions are made which, if abstracted from the narrative within which agents make their decisions, seem to be self-defeating. This is already to deny that they act with the type of rationality assumed by rational choice theory, for agents act historically. They are part of a world which has constituted them, but which in turn they participate in and change through their purposive actions. The consensus within which they act is neither external nor static. In changing outcomes the identity of the agent is transformed. We would consider it insane for the British state to claim that it will re-conquer its former Empire in its entirety in the next five years. It would be a denial of the external constraints on the will and the existence of others, an understanding that fundamentally affects the identity of the agent and does not simply function as an external constraint.

Politics, especially during periods of transformation, is a struggle over the terms of definition of that world, an argument over what is and what is not unalterable in it.[24] Such an understanding frames the rationality of politics. If the revolutionary fallacy can be defined as the belief that all forms of social relations can be transformed simultaneously, ignoring the essential continuity of materials and understandings that exist through time, then the social scientific fallacy is that agents act within a fixed rationality that is not itself the site of a struggle over re-definition. A change in a consensus is not only the reformulation of interests in transformed material circumstances through a realignment of power relations, but is a change in the understanding of the world held by the participants. This transforms the identity of the agents and the definition of interests and rationality. The definition of the world accepted as unavoidable by agents is the starting point for the analysis developed here, for unless the ways in which agents interpret the world are understood it would be impossible to

---

23. Evil is a problem for all theories of rational action. It will be supposed here that what makes evil effective is duplicity and such dishonesty always has to pay homage to that which it despises or cheats. In order to be successful evil has to disguise itself. See Immanuel Kant, *Religion Within the Limits of Reason Alone*, New York 1960, section one.

24. See chapter one, pp. 5–19.

understand why they act in certain ways. The 'way of the world' is the definition of reality given by the prevailing institutionalized consensus within which agents live and work.

The context, the material conditions within and upon which agents act, is itself defined by consensus. For example, one could be surrounded by coal. If there is no knowledge of what it is, or could be, one might as well be surrounded by rock. Similarly, one could be in a context characterized by developed industry and skilled workers; if all one sees is the perverse outcome of state socialism and an undeveloped service sector one might as well be surrounded by rust. It is with the prevailing consensus which informs the rationality of the dominant agents that the theory of agency developed here begins. A consensus gives meaning both to 'objective' context and to 'subjective' action.

The reason for stressing these points is given by the necessity of preserving the agent (whether individual, co-operative, communal or collective) as having a rationality, yet at the same time recognizing that the inherited consensus acts as a constraint on the types of action that can be meaningfully affirmed as rational.

The example used in chapter one to indicate the connection between agency, consensus and reason is the capacity of the state to reduce unemployment. Keynes argued that the unemployment level of the 1920s was the result of the inadequacy of the prevailing economic doctrine of self-regulating markets.[25] The state controlled the money supply within an economy, it set tax levels, it thus had the power to sponsor counter-cyclical public works. This distributed purchasing power to those whose spending needs were most immediate by provoking consumer demand as a means of reactivating industrial production and reducing unemployment. By redefining the possibilities for state intervention within market systems, the terms of political rationality were transformed. The New Deal in the United States in the 1930s incorporated a Keynesian definition of economic rationality in as much as political decision was explicitly recognized as enjoying an endogenous role in determining economic outcomes. Central to Roosevelt's justification of the dollar devaluation in 1933 was a rejection of 'the old fetishes of so called international bankers', and the subordination of the principles of monetary orthodoxy to the demands

---

25. See J.M. Keynes, *A Treatise on Money*, Vol. 2, London 1930.

of national economic recovery.[26] Abstract academic ideas concerning the status of spontaneous equilibrium, utility and money as a commodity had a practical effect on political realities. The verdict of capital markets was challenged by the rationality of democratic power.

The New Right project of the 1980s was, above all, a reassertion of market sovereignty in the organization of the economy. It was argued that interference by the state within the complex self-regulating market system of extended economic exchange creates greater unemployment and government authoritarianism in the long term. The power to define the value of currency was re-transferred from Washington to New York and London. Human beings had to take their place alongside raw materials as a factor of production in a just and prosperous society.

It was argued in chapter one that it is in the exclusion of alternatives to a consensus as 'insane' that the power of agenda-setting is most effective. A societal consensus is an understanding of the world shared by its principal agents which clusters around common assumptions concerning the person, rationality and history. This results in significant, durable institutions concerned with the distribution of power and goods within society. Institutions embody a moral philosophy and a distinctive rationality which form the philosophical underpinnings of a political consensus and are expressed and enforced by the state.[27]

The 'stagflation' of the 1970s, as well as the failure of the Mitterrand non-experiment, the interminable 'Crisis of the Swedish model' and the dense vacuity of Ordo-liberalism, led to the development of a widespread consensus that the post-war settlement was incapable of renewing itself. There was social struggle but very little political argument. Christian and Social Democrats were incapable of resisting the New Right on rational or moral terms. The victory of the New Right was ultimately conceptual.

The importance of a consensus as both a constraint on and a constituent of action is not only to be understood as an external

---

26. In this case in order to support agricultural prices. Quoted in Arrighi p. 279. Also see J.A. Frieden, *Banking on the World: The Politics of American International Finance*, New York 1987, p. 55. What Polanyi called the 'dispossession of Wall Street' was the precondition of pursuing New Deal policies. TGT, p. 229.

27. See MacIntyre, *After Virtue*, p. 194. Also chapter one, pp. 5–19.

imposition but as the necessary starting point of historical investigation. A challenge to the prevailing institutional interpretations of reality, is also a crisis of social relations. It is at this point that the methodology of the social sciences takes on a political and ideological form.

Crisis, Narrative and Political Change

Paradigms and narrative

There are various terms used to describe the most general shared framework through which people interpret the world and participate in society: paradigm, ideology, culture, language game, *Weltanschauung*, form of life, world-view, presupposition, myth, *mentalité*, *Sinnzusammenhänge*, consensus. Paradigm is the term used here as it is a particular type of theory which is directly related to practical activity due to its necessary features of shared understandings and institutionalized practices. These act as a means of defining rules, establishing norms and achieving results. Paradigms are definitionally linked to achievements. 'Real existing socialism' and 'welfare capitalism', as they existed in Europe since the war, were linked to Marxist and Keynesian paradigms respectively. A mode of societal regulation becomes a paradigm when theoretical speculation and disciplinary practices (daily work and organization) form a coherent, or at least a functioning, unity. A paradigm links modes of activity with models of explanation. This refers as much to welfare state regimes as it does to scientific communities. Some theory is necessarily prior to hard fact, otherwise we would not know what to define as important or insignificant. Specific modes of understanding which create institutional structures, communities of adherents and workable predictive hypotheses are those types of theory that successfully select and order these facts. Paradigms are thus institutionally enforced modes of understanding with an internal commitment to reason.

Paradigms give a starting point for analysing historical processes and structures which is given neither by subjective cognition and interests (the individual), nor objective conditions (structure), but by the dominant and prevailing institutional interpretation of what is important in the world, what counts as evidence and success. A paradigm is a form of revisable historically institutionalized explanation, the rationality of which is tied to its predictive power and relative explanatory coherence. These explanations necessarily take a narrative form when they vindicate themselves relative to competing paradigms (in this case ideologies) as a distinctive institutional practice.

The overall coherence and effectiveness of paradigm credibility is given by the integration of its premises and assumptions with a plausible account of its predictive successes and failures. Narratives provide an alternative and superior form of explanation to formal models, for they can include a comparative examination of evidence, process and history in a way that an abstract mathematical formula cannot. The foundational role that narrative plays in reason is particularly important when analysing crisis and transition, for it provides a conscious historical account of how it is that one large-scale paradigm can engage with another in cases where each paradigm embodies its own conception of what rational superiority consists of.[28] Narrative links historical events to causal assumptions. They impose order, rank events and render meaningful what threatens to become a disconnected barrage of disjointed facts.

Crisis and reconstruction: the history of science

An example of narrative importance in economic theory is the role that 'market failure' played in causing the great depression. For Keynes, the market failed because classical economic theory had no means of conceptualizing the state as a rational economic actor. He argued that it had a necessary role in a functioning market economy due to its control of monetary policy and taxation. The state was rendered impotent by the inadequacy of economic orthodoxy. The importance of the New Deal was that it restored legitimacy to direct economic involvement of the state in the productive economy.[29] For Friedman it was not the market but the state that caused the crash. The erratic performance of the Federal

---

28. Kuhn, *Structure of Scientific Revolutions*, chapters five to nine. The reason why the concept of paradigm is used here (and not theory) is precisely that paradigms refer to concerted practical activity.

29. See Arrighi, pp. 266–81. Also see Franz Schurmann, *The Logic of World Power: An Inquiry into the Origins, Currents and Contradictions of World Politics*, New York 1974, p. 71.

Reserve Bank and bureaucratic competition with the Economic Ministry led to what was falsely understood as a market failure.[30] The clash between the New Right and Old Left was not over morality but historical explanation.

Narratives are usually implicit and do not need explication each time a challenge is made to them. Everyday life involves a myriad of tacit assumptions which only a social scientist or existentialist would continuously question.[31] Anomalies within lived paradigms, however, can lead to levels of disorientation capable of undermining the most basic preconditions of intelligible action. The world can become incomprehensible. When this incoherence becomes incapable of either enduring or incrementally transforming itself, breakdown occurs. A breakdown is an immanent possibility for any identity, whether it be individual, communal, co-operative, corporate, conceptual or collective. Whether it be a private multinational corporation or a political party, an ideology or a religion. What is true for any identity also holds for a conceptual scheme and thus breakdown is an immanent possibility for any political paradigm.

When a previously functional or uncontested shared conceptual framework fragments, an agent can simultaneously experience an identity crisis and an epistemological breakdown. Crisis was earlier defined as (a) an 'anomaly overload' in which the previous mode of understanding and action has its functional efficiency undermined by information which it can neither explain nor deny, leading to a decline in credibility. A crisis was also defined as (b) transient. It is a mode of confusion to which a solution must be found. For example, a Keynesian believed that state intervention in the market led to economic growth, inflation and reduced unemployment, or to increased unemployment, falling inflation and slower growth. The state acts on these assumptions, but the result is greater unemployment, slower growth and inflation. An anomaly emerged which could not be explained by the theory. Evidence that seemed to point in only one direction opens itself,

---

30. See M. Friedman and A.J. Schwartz, *A Monetary History of the United States 1867-1960*, New Jersey 1963. For an exemplar of narrative re-ordering as applied to the supersession of Keynesian by Monetarist paradigms, see M. Friedman, 'The Counter Revolution in Monetary Theory', Paper 33, IEA, London 1970.
31. See Michael Polanyi, *Personal Knowledge*, London 1958.

through its inability to explain data, to rival interpretations as the agent is forced to consider other explanations as a means of rendering the world more amenable to understanding. The agent may realize at moments such as this that they have been deceived and be overwhelmed by the divergent character of alternative interpretations.[32]

This is first expressed as a crisis of trust. The agent does not know who to believe. If a previously persuasive and functional form of life breaks down then the agent experiences this crisis of trust in the form of the question 'Who can I trust?' At this point the competing and conflicting interpretations that exist in the world are both acknowledged and compound the crisis. This is related to a crisis of authority. If the previous authorities on whom reasonable action depended have either been shown to be fools or liars, then there is a corresponding breakdown in the social bonds that previously maintained and mobilized solidarity and trust.[33] If the previously held truths are now undermined, how can the agent believe in anything any more? This is potentially debilitating because until we know what to treat as evidence, we can have no scheme of interpretation, but until we have a scheme of interpretation we can have no evidence. There can be no appeal in these cases to neutral and independent data given by observation, for the perception and identification of relevant data depend on the paradigm which orders the understanding. Until we know what is and is not important in any particular context we will not know what to do. The general crisis can be summarized by Marvin Gaye's first question of sociology: 'What's going on?', which is logically and conceptually prior to Lenin's question of 'What is to be done?'[34]

It is at this general level of crisis that the importance of narrative reconstruction is vital, for it re-orders the understanding of the past and thus facilitates future-oriented action by making sense of the present. Through a plausible interpretation of a previous crisis,

---

32. The analysis developed here draws upon Alasdair MacIntyre, 'Epistemological Crisis. Dramatic Narrative and the Philosophy of Science', *The Monist*, Vol. 4, 1977, pp. 453–72.

33. It is held to be axiomatic that human beings cannot bear to live according to the maxim of groundless bullshit. If they did, there would never be any problems at all, as they would not mind eating and living in it as well.

34. Marvin Gaye, *What's Going On?*, Detroit 1972. Vladimir Lenin, *What is to be Done?*, New York 1902.

trust, intelligibility and truth are restored, although in a modified form. The modification being that a revision of the present solution is always possible. When an epistemological crisis is resolved, a new narrative emerges which enables an agent to understand both how a person could intelligibly have held their original beliefs and how they could have been misled by them. There has to be an understanding of what was wrong with the previous explanation before any stable new understanding can be affirmed.[35]

Concept, conception and tradition

The New Right, Left and Centre all are aspects of a political tradition which is here understood as the democratic control of the state in order to pursue policies that will maximise freedom. None of the agents in the intellectual and political debate over the crisis of the post-war settlement in the 1970s rejected the importance of justice and democracy. This is a logical point which can be made in the following way:

1. Two theories offer conflicting interpretations of the world.
2. These theories are understood by themselves and by others as rivals.
3. Therefore, they must have a shared concept about which they agree, for otherwise they could not communicate their disagreement to themselves or others. The conflict over the agenda does not lead to political incommensurability of values.[36]

There are *concepts*, shared abstract categories of thought which define a domain of meaning designated by a word, and there are *conceptions*, which refer to different interpretations of that meaning. Ideologies, as embodied in the institutions of societal regulation, are a particular recombination of these concepts. Since the major ideological paradigms have been in place for more than a hundred years, and therefore have transformed themselves in relation to each other through time, paradigms can also be seen as

35. Imre Lakatos, 'Falsification and the Methodology of Scientific Research Programmes', in I. Lakatos and A. Musgrave, eds, *Criticism and the Growth of Knowledge*, Cambridge 1970, pp. 91–196, p. 119.

36. The concept of incommensurability used here refers to the different perspectives of paradigms not of values.

agents. They have institutions, adherents, victories and defeats. A theory or a paradigm, in the words of Lakatos, is always a 'growing developing entity, one which cannot be considered as a static structure'.[37] The definition of utility found in economics textbooks will be different in 1848, 1948, 1979, and 1990.[38] The theory of utility is best understood as the history of a theory, the record of a series of encounters with confirming or anomalous evidence, with other theories and with philosophical developments.

The plurality of truth and the singularity of lies

The gap between the story we now believe and that which was superseded is a gap of falsity.[39] To evaluate a paradigm is to evaluate the series of theories that make it up, its narrative of successes and defeats, and the responses to these experiences. There is no theory-independent way to understand the world, but there are rival theories which give better or worse explanations from within the rationality of a paradigm, defined as the dynamic tradition within which thought can be expressed and communicated concerning practical activity. That is why Bolshevik economics no longer exists as a theory. It has ceased to function as a rational theory of collective action or managerial efficiency. Hirst and Zeitlin summarize this view when they write:

> Competing interpretations, like competing theories more generally, can properly be ranked in terms of their plausibility in accounting for agreed features of a common body of evidence according to internally consistent criteria.[40]

The truth is plural as it seeks to link facts into an explanatory whole by telling a plausible causal story. Lies are singular, in that

---

37. Imre Lakatos, 'History of Science and Rational Reconstructions', in Roger C. Buch and Robert S. Cohen, eds, *Boston Studies in the Philosophy of Science*, Vol. 8, Dortrecht 1974.

38. In 1848 it would involve a static calculation of cost with fixed dependants, in 1990 it would incorporate dynamic interaction in uncertain conditions with weighted variables. It is still utility defined as a rational calculation of the best possible outcome.

39. The consensus-based form of enquiry developed here holds that the discontinuity between theory[T] at $time[t]^1$ and Tt^2 is given, in necessary part, by the elimination of central aspects of Tt^1, and that reasons can be given for that transition. It is a retrospective theory of falsity.

40. Hirst and Zeitlin, 'Flexible Specialisation', p. 35.

they are isolatable and false. An example of this is given by the Soviet invasion of Lithuania in 1939. For over forty years the Soviet state claimed that this event did not take place. The reasons for the Molotov-Ribbentrop pact are amenable to several true accounts. The appeasement policies of Great Britain and France, the Fascist tendencies in the Lithuanian government and the insecure position of Russians living there were all factors in explaining the Soviet decision. The plausibility of a narrative is predicated on the elimination of lies. The Soviet claim that there was no invasion in 1939 was false. The rationality of Soviet action was undermined by their propaganda.

The New Right, the New Left and the Crisis of Old Social Democracy

What the New Right succeeded in doing in the 1970s was to combine a set of previously disconnected theories in order to emphasize certain facts. This was done by redefining the problems generated by what they took to be the dominant institutionalized paradigm established after the Second World War and presented an alternative explanation of the 'crisis' of the 1970s and the measures necessary to effect its overcoming. Utilitarian calculation by the state was rejected as the primary activity of politics. The prevailing theory of history, defined as an incremental historical process of extending ever more substantive social rights as outlined in T.H. Marshall's evolutionary account of industrial society, was historically, morally and methodologically 'discredited'.[41] In doing so the role of the state was redefined. The libertarian criticism of Keynesian and socialist policy was combined with a communitarianism which could find embodiment only in a strong and renewed nation-state. In this new paradigm the unit of economic rationality, the meaning of politics and the content of justice were all redefined.

This was achieved by relocating reason in the individual; order and community were maintained by the state and family. The desirability of a market system was reconciled with the need for a strong moralistic state. The discipline required for enforcing

---

41. See T.H. Marshall, *Citizenship and Social Class*, London 1950.

contracts was a state responsibility and the conflicts which created the need for extended police powers were constantly re-created by market conditions. They were mutually necessary, not antagonistic, commitments.[42]

The New Right cast the events of the post-war years on both sides of Europe into a narrative. Nazism and socialism were seen as relatives of the same family of totalitarian ideologies. The only inviolable rights became those pertaining to private property and national self-determination. They distinguished between those features of the post-war settlement which were genuine challenges to the existing paradigm (regime undermining anomalies) and those which could be dealt with in an ad hoc manner as necessary features of any order (system independent variables, or more commonly: the way of the world). The New Right naturalized the market, moralized the state and sanctified the family as the elemental institutions in society. The fundamental problems of the post-war settlement were defined as bureaucratic domination, institutionalized trade-union power, democratic overload and the interference of non-economic factors in the functioning of market systems. This led to stagnation, inflation, government confusion and inter-systemic interference, combined with the repressive use of state coercive power; all processes occurring simultaneously.

The New Right defined itself against the prevailing mode of organization which, it was argued, could not address or understand these problems let alone solve them. Social Democracy's commitment to greater equality and active citizenship could not be reconciled with the passive unemployed mass of dependants its welfare system sustained.[43] The growth of bureaucratic interference perverted just allocation while creating the conditions of tyranny at worst, paternalism at best.[44] The cause of 'stagflation' was the arbitrary interference of the state in a spontaneous process which it could not possibly predict or control.[45] The fallibility of human knowledge, it was argued, entailed the recognition that the detailed central direction of economic and social life is unworkable as well as immoral. The New Right claimed that the

---

42. See chapter one.
43. See Charles Murray, *Losing Ground*, New York 1984.
44. Robert Nozick, *Anarchy, State and Utopia*, Oxford 1974.
45. See Hayek, *Errors*.

fragmentation of common interests could only be overcome by the appeal to a collective sense of nationality, not the partial solidarity of class.[46]

Conservatism moved from being a reactionary ideology to a self-consciously progressive political force through its critique of bureaucracy, stagnation and the perverse consequences that necessarily followed from post-war commitments to a welfare, productive and participatory state. They did this by appealing to both markets and order, rights and community. They took over the language of progress, entitlement and justice that had previously been alien territory and in this way undermined the rationality and identity of both Social Democracy and Marxism.[47] Problems of long-term waves of unemployment, recession and the corresponding waves of boom and prosperity were system-independent anomalies and were not structural problems of the capitalist system alone. There was no way of avoiding them, but equally there was no way of creating them either; they were the result of a spontaneous accumulation of individual choices which no guiding hand could predict or control.[48]

The New Right and Old Left were committed to the same things – justice, freedom and democratic community – it was simply that the Old Left was philosophically inept, methodologically backward and conceptually confused. The New Right were able to understand the problem of the prevailing institutional arrangement in a newly intelligible way. They enabled people to understand why the previous paradigm had to be rejected when compared with the practical and theoretical superiority of their prescriptions for preserving freedom and renewing society.

The political crisis: too much government, too little order

The New Right defined the crisis of the 1970s in economic, political and legal terms.[49] Each of these was subdivided in terms of cause and effect and on that basis a solution was proposed. The

---

46. Roger Scruton, *The Meaning of Conservatism*, London 1984.

47. The New Right not only transformed the understanding of the left, but the post-war settlement transformed the meaning of the right.

48. See Hayek section in chapter one, pp. 24–7.

49. See M.J. Crozier, S.P. Huntington and J. Watanuki, *The Crisis of Democracy: Report on the Governability of Democracies to the Trilateral Commission*, New York 1975.

political crisis was that of 'governability'. The demands made upon the state were escalating, leading to bureaucratic overload and confusion of functions. In Crozier's words, the paradoxical predicate of modern politics was that: 'While it has been traditionally believed that the power of the state depended on the number of decisions it could take, the more decisions a modern state has to handle, the more helpless it becomes.'[50]

The tax burden necessary for maintaining state growth led to excessive demands being made on the economic system. This served to weaken the incentive to innovate. The welfare state distorted labour supply and eroded managerial authority through state-constructed 'exit' opportunities in the form of unconditional unemployment benefit and housing subsidies. Vocational and educational institutions were defined as subordinate to entrepreneurial energy and technological update in the hierarchy of the causes of competitive success.

In a 'mixed' economy, the private sector was not only besieged by excessive redistributive demands through a tax system which penalized wealth creation while undermining market effectiveness, it also had to subsidize nationalized industries on which it was often dependent economically. State ownership of productive industries was viewed as necessarily inefficient, for there could be no take-over or valuation on a stock exchange. The state proved to be an unlimited supplier of subsidies, thus distorting competitive equilibrium. Privatization was seen as essential to both unburden government, free up markets and impose managerial discipline.[51] The state, conceived as a long-term economic planner, was seen as a methodological delusion. It was no longer an effective economic agent in the new international division of labour.[52] International competition rendered state plans unreliable and inappropriate. If workers could not produce at a competitive, internationally determined norm (the going rate) then unemployment was the natural outcome. National prosperity would be best served by buying elsewhere. In this way the demands made on governments not only to subsidize inefficient industries, which they owned, but to intervene

---

50. Ibid., p.13.
51. This was turned into political capital by selling state assets at below market rates to citizens while reducing the cost of government.
52. See David Gordon, 'The Global Economy: New Edifice or Crumbling Foundations', *New Left Review*, No. 168, 1988, pp. 24–65.

in order to save inefficient industries which they did not, would cease. Government overload would be eased. The sovereignty of the consumer lowered the tax burdens on the citizen.

The crisis of governability was not only created by state control of organizations it could not manage, its institutions were also open to forces who had no right to political participation. The politically significant point about the 'New Social Movements', against which the New Right defined their identity, was that they criticized the welfare state in ways similar to the New Right.[53] The New Left argued that the Social Democratic consensus led to stagnation, the bureaucratization of daily life, the colonization of the life world, it undermined the self-organized movements which were historically the social basis of the struggle to achieve justice which left socialism without an active constituency. The social market was seen as embodying an irreducible contradiction between welfare and the market.[54] Social Democracy was under siege from left and right, with the common ground of criticism bearing on the destruction of 'civil society' by the state.

By 1979 there were very few agents prepared to defend the post-war settlement. The New Right took the New Left analysis of the welfare state, added the economic stagnation caused by state ownership, the deleterious effects of progressive taxation on incentive structures and the privileges granted to the trade unions. The crisis of governability was related to these three aspects of state colonization by organized interests; overload through an expansion of welfare provision and public disorder.

The economic crisis: too much history

If the political crisis was one of order then the economic crisis was about stagnation. The model used to understand this malaise was given by renewed classical methodology which assumes certain things. The first is that markets consist of individual agents who spontaneously exchange goods and if left to their own devices

---

53. See L. Williams, 'Ideological Parallels between the New Left and New Right', *Social Science Journal*, Vol. 24, 1987, pp. 317–27.

54. The most influential expression of this is Claus Offe, *Contradictions of the Welfare State*, London 1984. He writes: 'What the state desires to do becomes evidently impossible to accomplish unless the private character of accumulation or the liberal democratic character of the polity are suspended' (p. 276).

achieve equilibrium in demand and supply through the medium of prices. The second is that the economic sphere is autonomous of society. The third is that agents act to maximize their advantage. Agent rationality is a fixed aspect of human nature which is characterized by choices governed by rules of utility maximization. The achievement of normative political goals through macroeconomic planning was seen as a core feature of Keynesian irrationality. The distinctiveness of the new ideology was the achievement of normative political goals through individual economic rationality. The individual became the locus of choice, the context of choice the market, the motivation self-interest. Any institutions mediating between the individual and the market caused distortions in price signals which undermined the spontaneous growth that would otherwise have been achieved.

The same logic of argument which led to the necessity of unmediated state authority in the form of rights also emptied the economy of institutions that could enmesh markets in local or vocational organizations. The problem was that although history was a vindication of the market, there was simply too much history cropping up in economic calculations. There was state control of the money supply and exchange controls which distorted value by protecting currencies from market forces. There was state control over industries which were both outside the market in terms of stock-exchange control and inside the market in terms of the sale of their products. There was a tax system which penalized 'wealth creators' the more they succeeded, there were welfare schemes which altered the workings of the labour market through creating rational choice unemployment. The post-war settlement was defined as an extensive system of racketeering in the form of price and wage fixing in labour, property and money. There was an excessive regulation of production which interfered with the autonomy of firms and there was institutionalized union power which granted an unwarranted economic advantage through their legal and political privileges.[55] There were too many contingent variables distorting the system. History interfered with a well-ordered economy, and in the economic sphere, history was methodologically abolished. A third period of market utopianism was inaugurated.

---

55. An account of how besieged the capitalist class felt itself to be in the 1960s and 1970s is made by Michael Useem, *The Inner Circle: Large Corporations and the Rise of Business Political Activity in the US and UK*, Oxford 1984.

6

Unnecessary Suffering

The Economics of Martial Law: 1981–1989

With its victory in 1989, Solidarity became the government party in Poland. Rationality, as defined by the prevailing international consensus, entailed the subordination of the substantive institutions of Polish society to the logic of formal economics. Land, labour and productive organizations were the three elements of Polish culture that required commodification. In 1945 Solidarity's ideas were characteristic of the post-war settlement. By 1989, any regulation of the commodity fictions was considered to be 'populist'. No societal institutions could find a constructive role within the austere methodological parameters of what became known as shock therapy.[1] This was continuous with the policies pursued by the previous Communist administration.

With the imposition of martial law in December 1981 the Ministry of Finance and the Central Bank became the primary instruments of macro-economic management. The Law on Economic Planning of 1982 abolished the five-year plan and shifted the management of the economy away from the party apparatus and branch bureaucracy. The Economic Activity Act of 1987–88 distributed further power to the enterprises through the creation of limited-liability companies, which by 1988 accounted

---

1. Leszek Balcerowicz was the main author of the stabilization plan and Minister of Finance and Deputy Prime Minister between 1989 and 1991. The term shock therapy was derived from his reading of the behavioural psychologist Leon Festinger's *A Theory of Cognitive Dissonance*, Chicago 1957, and his argument that human beings adapt faster to radical than to incremental change. Balcerowicz, p. 305.

for over one-fifth of Poland's economic activity, employing 1,288,000 people. Despite the growth of the private sector, 86.2 per cent of tax returns came from state enterprises which also donated the capital for the formation of the new private companies.[2] Employees' councils were abolished in these 'spontaneously' privatized companies which were also exempt from the tax on wage increases. The share of government expenditure on social welfare dropped from 22.9 per cent in 1981 to 20.8 per cent in 1988 and was lower in Poland than in any socialist country other than Romania.[3] Between 1980 and 1987 the number of injuries per 1,000 employees increased by a third and by 1989 every second worker died before they reached retirement.[4]

The lengthening of the working day, welfare cuts, enterprise autonomy and greater managerial prerogative imposed under martial law were to no avail. By 1989 the Polish debt had risen from $23.9 billion to $41.4 billion, despite the payment of $18 billion to Western creditors.[5] By 1986, the debt constituted 43 per cent of GNP and was five times the amount of annual hard currency earnings. In 1987 the government declared that Poland would 'implement all the IMF recommendations on economic policy' and announced the 'Programme for the Second Stage of Economic Reform'.[6] This called for currency convertibility, high interest rates, a liberalization of prices and an increase in privatization. The government consequently raised prices on foodstuffs, devalued the zloty and substantially reduced subsidies to state enterprises.[7] The response was a wave of rolling strikes throughout the Baltic coast. As in 1970, 1976 and 1980, the leadership of the government changed and talks were announced with Solidarity in February

---

2. Tittenbrun, p. 140.
3. Tittenbrun, p.122.
4. Tittenbrun, p. 97.
5. The sanctions imposed on the Jaruzelski regime did not apply to debt.
6. *Zycie Gospodarcze*, No. 38, 1987, p. 1.
7. See Stanislaw Owsiak, 'Financial Crisis of the Polish State', in Jerzy Hausner, Bob Jessop and Klaus Nielson, eds, *Strategic Choice and Path-Dependency in Post-Socialism: Institutional Dynamics in the Transformation Process*, Aldershot 1995 (hereafter Owsiak), pp. 149–67, p. 154. Also see S. Ryszard Domanski, 'The Quest for Ownership: Why it was so easy to break communism, and why it is so difficult to find social consensus: A response to the "Surprise Literature"', *Eastern European Economics*, Vol. 32, No. 2, 1994, pp. 71–94 (hereafter Domanski), p. 81.

1989. While these were taking place an act was passed which granted the Finance Ministry overriding administrative powers in order to 'increase the pace of reform'. This was followed by a second announcement by the outgoing government that all state enterprises were to be turned into joint-stock companies owned by the Ministry of Finance.[8] This was followed by the withdrawal of state subsidies for food products in August 1989 which led to a sevenfold increase in prices.[9]

Solidarity developed a different conception of how the burdens of transformation should be distributed. During the Round Table negotiations an agreement was reached which was consistent with both the Gdansk Accord and the Solidarity document of 1981.[10] The *Position Concerning Social and Economic Policy and the Reform of the Socio-Economic System*, called for the development of employee self-management, the establishment of works councils in each large company whether public or private, and 'constitutional guarantees' of employee participation in the management of all firms.[11] The *Position* document provided the manifesto upon which Solidarity, led by Tadeusz Mazowiecki, contested the election of June 1989. It won ninety nine of the hundred available seats in the Senate.

The Economics of Stabilization: 1989–1996

Justice as fairness, enterprise democracy and the self-governing republic did not, however, become the policy of the new Solidarity government. They proposed, in contrast, a programme that differed little from the 'Second Stage of Economic Reform'. The 'stabilization' plan consisted of six policies: privatization; taxes on wages in the public sector; high interest rates; the abolition of trade restrictions; the convertibility of the zloty, and the abolition

---

8. Kowalik writes that: 'This was nothing more than an attempt to eliminate all employee councils at one blow, while bringing these companies under even greater state control than before.' Tadeusz Kowalik, 'Reply to Maurice Glasman', *New Left Review*, No. 206, 1994, p. 138 (hereafter Reply).

9. Tittenbrun, p. 94.

10. See chapter four.

11. Reply, p. 137.

of price controls.[12] There were two methods of privatization proposed. The first was 'liquidation' in which the firm was either sold or leased out to a new owner.[13] The second was 'commercialization'. This involved the transformation of the largest state enterprises into limited-liability companies in which the Finance Ministry owned all the stock.[14] In short, after 1989 the state embarked on a programme of nationalization. The most significant change resulting from this form of privatization was the abolition of the works councils and the state appointment of the supervisory board who were to be paid at six times the average wage.[15] Commercialization thus strengthened managerial authority within the enterprise, reintroduced the nomenklatura system and increased differentials without establishing private ownership.[16] The state became the enterprise owner as well as tax collector, privatizing agency and political authority. Far from removing itself from the power structure of the firm, the state appeared more pervasively than before. As Polanyi wrote of nineteenth-century market utopianism, 'The road to the free market was opened and kept open by an enormous increase in continuous, centrally organized and controlled interventionism.'[17]

It is consistent with the argument made in chapter one that the market would be imposed by the state. The Solidarity government

12. For a detailed account of the policy measures see Dariusz Chelminski, Andrzej A. Czynzyk and Henryk Sterniczuk, 'New Forms of State Ownership in Poland: The Case of Commercialization' in G.S. Alexander and G. Skapska, eds, *A Fourth Way? Privatization, Property and the Emergence of New Market Economies*, London 1994, pp. 182–97, p. 184.

13. This accounts for 76 per cent of privatization, a third of which are worker buy outs. See Maria Jarosz, ed., *Employee-Owned Companies in Poland*, Warsaw 1994. The overwhelming majority of these 'liquidations' were, in fact, bankruptcies. See Jerzy Hausner, *Populist Threat in Transformation of Socialist Society*, Warsaw 1992, p. 13 (hereafter Hausner).

14. Chelminski, 'New Forms of State Ownership', p. 187.

15. The first Minister of Privatization, Janusz Lewandowski justified this on the grounds that it is 'economically reasonable to rely on managers'. Chelminski, 'New Forms of State Ownership', p. 194. Also see Domanski, pp. 85–6.

16. One of the effects of privatization was that government subsidies to state enterprises rose from 1.9 per cent in 1988 to 12.7 per cent by the end of 1990. OECD, *Industry in Poland: Structural Adjustment Issues and Policy Options*, Paris 1992, p. 30 (hereafter OECD). By the end of 1994, only 100 enterprises had been privatized through commercialization.

17. TGT, p. 140. See also Domanski, pp. 86–7.

had an unprecedented degree of popular authority and legitimacy. There were also no social forces capable of organizing resistance.[18] The logic of the government was to impose new economic rules without public discussion.[19] There was no place for negotiation in the definition of the common good or the distributions of burdens required for transformation. Shock therapy bypassed the need to negotiate common rules between societal agents by evoking the authority of economic science. As Hausner describes it, 'The programme itself was from the outset beyond the sphere of social discourse, beyond debate.'[20] The economic liberals and the reformed Communists both focused on the Ministry of Finance as the motor of reform, thus subordinating industrial policy to the demands of currency convertibility.[21] Nuti records that in December 1989, the letter of intent to the IMF outlining the basic policies of shock therapy was distributed to the non-economic Cabinet ministers with blank spaces for figures, the substance of the agreement already agreed.[22] On 30 December the Balcerowicz plan was signed by President Wojciech Jaruzelski and passed by the

18. The Communist Party was more concerned with survival and reorientation. The Peasants' Party initially assumed that the reforms would be to its benefit and the OPZZ was unsure of its status. After 1989 Solidarity's membership was two million, one-fifth of its 1981 level. Only 20 of the 250 Solidarity representatives in the Sejm signed a petition opposing the Balcerowicz plan. See Alexander Surdej, 'Politics and the Stabilisation Plan', Cracow Academy of Economics Seminar Paper No. 9, 1992, p. 33 (hereafter Surdej).

19. See Tadeusz Kowalik, 'The Free Market or a Social Contract as Bases of Systemic Transformation', in Jerzy Hausner, Bob Jessop and Klaus Nielson, eds, *Strategic Choice and Path-Dependency in Post-Socialism: Institutional Dynamics in the Transformation Process*, Aldershot 1995, pp. 131–48, p. 135.

20. Hausner, p. 70.

21. An analysis of the Polish state concludes that it is characterized by a 'total control of the economy by the finance ministry'. See Joanna J. Mizgala, 'The Ecology of Transformation: The Impact of the Corporate State on the Development of the Party system in Poland, 1989–93', *East European Politics and Society*, Vol. 8, No. 2, 1993, pp. 358–68, p. 360. For the alliance between reform communists and neo-classical academics see Domanski, p. 84. Also see Balcerowicz, p. 303.

22. See Mario Nuti, 'Lessons from Polish Stabilisation', Paper, Trieste, 1991, p. 24. The programme was initially presented in Washington and drawn up in cooperation with the IMF. For an account of how the *Position* document was abandoned see Waldemar Kuczynski, *Wyznania Zausznika*, Warsaw 1992. Even the IMF was surprised by the enthusiasm with which its model was adopted. See Michael Bruno, 'Stabilisation and Reform in Eastern Europe: A Preliminary Evaluation', IMF Working Paper WP/92/30, Washington DC 1992.

Communist-dominated Sejm.[23] The economics of martial law had become the policy of the new Solidarity government.

After 1989, the burdens of transformation were paid disproportionally by the working poor.[24] A drastic decline in real wages was accompanied by a doubling of those living below the poverty line.[25] According to the calculations of the World Bank, the decline in output between 1990 and 1991 was at a rate exceeding that of Germany and the US in the great depression.[26] In 1990 GDP declined by 11.6 per cent and sold industrial production in state-owned enterprises fell by a third.[27] From this level, by the end of 1991 production had fallen by a further 12 per cent.[28] Real wages declined by some 35 per cent from the beginning of 1990 to the end of 1992.[29] Unemployment rose from virtually zero to 1,126,000 in 1990, increasing to 2,108,000 by the end of 1991.[30] In short there was a 30 per cent decline in real wages, a 25 per cent decrease in national income, 15 per cent unemployment, fiscal collapse and an increase in foreign debt despite the remission for good behaviour granted by the Paris Club.[31] The only glimmer of hope lay in the self-managed state enterprises whose positive trade balance offset the deficit of the private sector.[32] These firms,

---

23. See Balcerowicz, p. 297.

24. If the poverty line is set at $86 a month, 27 per cent of Poles, some ten million people, were living below the poverty line by 1991. The highest concentration of poverty is found in those of working age. See *World Bank Report on Poverty in Poland: Vol. 1*, Washington 1994, p. 40 (hereafter World Bank).

25. The percentage of the Polish population suffering from mild malnutrition (less than 2,300 calories) rose to 17.9 per cent. Peter Gowan, 'Neo-Liberal Theory and Practice for Eastern Europe', *New Left Review*, No. 213, 1995, pp. 3–60, p. 22 (hereafter Gowan).

26. See World Bank, p. 1.

27. OECD, p. 17.

28. Poland's GDP in 1993 was at 1975 levels. World Bank, p. xi.

29. This is a low estimate, the OECD claim that it was 50 per cent, p. 78. See also Jan Adam, 'The Transition to a Market Economy in Poland', *Cambridge Journal of Economics*, Vol. 18, 1994, pp. 607–18, p. 611. Wage levels, in real terms, at the end of the Gomulka reforms in 1969, were at the level of twenty-five years before.

30. The suicide rate in Poland increased by 133 per cent between 1989 and 1993. UNICEF, *Economies in Transition Studies, Regional Monitoring Report, 1994. Crisis in Mortality, Health and Nutrition*, Florence 1994, p. 53.

31. Some 70 per cent of the Polish national debt was to Western governments and this was halved in recognition of the thoroughness of the stabilization plan.

32. For the inefficiency of the private sector see Owsiak, pp. 152–3. Also see Domanski, p. 88.

however, were the principal targets of the stabilization plan.

The 115 largest enterprises in Poland provided 52 per cent of employment, 60 per cent of exports and contributed 84 per cent of the budget. Discriminatory taxes were imposed so that they operated under significantly inferior conditions to those pertaining in the private sector.[33] A rent on firm assets (*dividenda*) and a tax on wage increases above the stipulated level (*popiwek*) were levied exclusively on state firms.[34] This penalized the more modern firms and forced a decline in wages irrespective of enterprise performance.[35] Firm debt reached record levels.[36] Of the 1,658 enterprises under direct state control, more than 750 were behind in their payments in July 1991, compared to 350 in January of the same year. Some 450 did not pay the *dividenda* and 170 were simply bankrupt and did not pay other firms or the state.[37] This was compounded by a rise in unit costs, most particularly energy prices, a drastic shrinking of markets as domestic demand collapsed along with trade with the ex-CMEA (Common Monetary and Economic Area) countries, and the pressure from imports.[38] Tariffs were lifted on some 80 per cent of the 5,000 items on the customs list.[39] Poland was subsequently glutted with imports from east and west which virtually doubled between 1989 and 1991 across all sectors.[40] The EU negotiated advantageous terms in areas of Eastern

---

33. Balcerowicz, p. 299.

34. In 1990 wage rises in the state sector were set at 30 per cent of the inflation rate in January, 20 per cent for the next three months and 60 per cent for the rest of the year. State owned enterprises were liable for tax penalties of 200–500 per cent on any increase above these levels. See Adam, pp. 610–11. Also, Kazimierz Kloc 'Polish Labour in Transition: 1990–1992', *Telos*, No. 92, 1992, pp. 139–48, p. 140.

35. OECD, p. 76. In the first year of reforms, productivity in state enterprises, as measured by net output per employee, was almost twice as high as that in the private sector. *Tygodnik Solidarnosc*, No. 8, 1990, p. 14.

36. By 1991 a third of GDP was made up of firm debt. See Hausner, p. 81.

37. OECD, p. 81.

38. The collapse of trade with the Soviet Union hit electronics and pharmaceuticals whose exports dropped by 22.2 per cent and 10.8 per cent respectively after 1989. Poland's exports to Western countries consisted of substantially low value added products, with the exception of shipbuilding. Food and raw materials provided the main hard currency earnings. OECD, p. 155.

39. For the extent of trade liberalization see P. Murrell, 'What is Shock Therapy? What did it do in Poland and Russia?', *Post-Soviet Affairs*, Vol. 9, No. 2, 1993, pp. 111–40.

40. OECD, p. 25.

European export strength, most particularly agriculture.[41]

Treasury policy led directly to state bankruptcy. In 1991, despite substantial reductions in welfare spending, the Polish government spent 11 per cent more than it raised in revenues.[42] Although the Polish Ministry of Finance anticipated a 15 per cent decline in expenditure for 1991, its revenues dropped by 22 per cent.[43] The dilemma of shock therapy was that while the entire programme of economic reform was based on the privatization of the state enterprises, these enterprises provided the basis of state finance.[44] Although 20 per cent of production was in private hands by early 1991, revenues from the private sector contributed only 5 per cent of the state budget.[45] Tax avoidance and cheating became common business practice.[46] The World Bank reported that the self-employed, if measured by spending power, are the richest group in Poland. In terms of taxable income receipts, however, they officially subsist on an income 30 per cent below those eligible for welfare benefit.[47] For all the rigours of shock therapy the Polish budget deficit rose further in 1992.[48] The effect of discriminating against the productive organizations of Polish society was thus fiscal collapse. Polanyi wrote that the ascendancy of economic rationalism led 'to the eclipse of political thought'.[49] Statecraft

---

41. See Patrick A. Messerlin, 'The Association Agreements between the EC and Central Europe: Trade Liberalism Vs Constitutional Failure?', in J. Flemming and J.M.C. Rollo, eds, *Trade, Payments and Adjustment in Central and Eastern Europe*, London 1992. For the decline in agricultural trade relations between Poland and the EU, see OECD, *Agricultural Policies, Markets and Trade. Monitoring and Outlook 1994*, Paris 1994.

42. Grzegorz Kolodko and Danuta Gotz-Kozierkiewicz, 'Fiscal Adjustment and Stabilization Policies in Eastern Europe', *Oxford Review of Economic Policy*, Vol. 8, No. 1, 1993, p. 20.

43. Kolodko, 'Fiscal Adjustment', p. 17.

44. The *popiwek* and *dividenda* contributed 20 per cent of the state budget. David Ost, 'Shock Therapy and its Discontents', *Telos*, No. 92, 1992, pp. 107–12, p. 110.

45. Tax receipts for private employees were 10 per cent of those in the public sector. See John L. Campbell, 'The Fiscal Crisis of Post-Communist States', *Telos*, No. 93, 1992, pp. 89–110, p. 109.

46. Setting aside the discounts, concessions and exemptions enjoyed by the private sector, many businessmen became skilled in forgery, evasion and fictitious transfers. Owsiak, p. 163. Campbell, p. 100.

47. World Bank, p. 17.

48. See Surdej, p. 36. Gowan, p. 29.

49. *Livelihood*, p. 14. See chapter one, pp. 5–19.

was abandoned after 1989 in favour of a policy which under-mined the conditions under which the state could fulfil its statutory and constitutional obligations.[50] The pursuit of market reforms led to a neglect of the values and institutions necessary for its mainte-nance.

International Consensus: 1945–1989

The policy prescriptions propounded by the institutions of inter-national economic governance played a critical role in defining what could be achieved through concerted political action.[51] The European Union became indistinguishable from the IMF, World Bank or United States in its policy prescriptions and there was thus no institutional or ideological competition in the interna-tional sphere. The balance of power had broken down. The EU handed over its aid budget to the IMF which thereby controlled the total aid given by the G-24 as well as the terms of debt repay-ment.[52] The ideological meaning of 'Europe' did not include economic democracy, it barely included a welfare state. Aid and advice focused almost exclusively on financial probity and a con-vertible currency as preconditions of economic integration. The terms of 'transition' were set by what was considered the most suc-cessful and rational means of achievement and on this the IMF and the Finance Ministry were in agreement.[53] It is the definition of what it is rational to pursue that led Solidarity to negate their pre-vious commitments and to revise their economic policy. Balcerowicz argued that shock therapy was based on 'proven mod-els which we know of from real market economies'.[54] A myth and three fictions thus came to be adopted in Poland in the name of rationality. The fictions were the commodity status of human

---

50. It was a classic instance of what Hayek referred to as 'constructivist ratio-nalism' in which the traditions and practices of society are subordinated to the plan of a centralized state. See chapter one, pp. 19–28.

51. Owsiak, pp. 186–7.

52. See Mario Nuti, 'Lessons from Polish Stabilisation', Paper, Trieste, 1991.

53. Balcerowicz writes that 'in negotiations with the IMF, multilateral banks and Western Governments, there was very little pressure with respect to economic strat-egy and its crucial details because the Polish programme was basically in line with the goals of these organisations', p. 310.

54. Balcerowicz, p. 343.

beings, nature and money; the myth was that these were the foundations of post-war European prosperity.

The problem for Solidarity was that of how to conceptualize its productive role within these constraints. The dilemma of representing the interests of a class and providing the social basis of state power was resolved by upholding a conception of the common good which was predicated upon the elimination of Solidarity's social base. Due to the model of economic reconstruction assumed by the Sachs-Balcerowicz-IMF plan, the only task it could effectively fulfil was to dissolve itself as an economic agent, while acting as a societal pacifier as the suffering and dislocation caused by the 'stabilization' plan took effect. While Solidarity was a necessary force in political reform, it viewed itself as a parasitic and obstructive organization in the economic sphere.[55] This assumption led Walesa to argue that 'If I build a strong union, I will be building an obstacle to reform'.[56]

One of Polanyi's arguments developed through his analysis of the Speenhamland scale is that the desolation of society in the name of its protection is a necessary condition for the imposition of market utopianism. Bolshevism had an effect on Polish culture similar to that of Speenhamland in England. It not only led to the pauperization of the self-sufficient, the erosion of personal morality and the destruction of work ethics, it also deprived labour of the capacity to legally associate. In 1834 as in 1989, the assault on the elements of society was irresistible. The abolition of Speenhamland was welcomed as an act of freedom in England just as Solidarity initially embraced market utopianism as a means of achieving their liberation from Communism.

An institutional comparison with post-war Germany is instructive. In both cases political parties had been banned and the state administration was implicated in the old regime. The Polish working class had traditions of militancy and democratic self-organization that parallel the labour movement in Germany in their resistance to both state and market.[57] Solidarity had been

---

55. The linkage of politics to economics through any other means than the money supply was forbidden.

56. Quoted in Surdej, p. 33.

57. The tactic of round-the-clock sit-down strikes was developed by Polish textile workers in 1931. See Maria Ciechocinska, *Polozenie klasy robotniczej w Polsce 1929–1939*, Warsaw 1965, pp. 145–6. Also see Laba, *The Roots of Solidarity*, pp. 101–4.

joined during martial law by the officially sponsored union, the Polish Confederation of Trade Unions (OPZZ), established in 1983. The split union is a difference with West Germany in which sectoral monopoly unions were encouraged by both state and owners. Property rights were ill-defined and uncertain in both cases. In Poland, the ownership of industries was disputed between individual factories, industrial sectors, previous owners, the state and work councils. In Germany they were owned exclusively by the occupying powers with strict demands for decartelization laid down in the Potsdam Agreement. The Catholic Church was as morally respected in Poland as it was in West Germany.

Three considerable differences emerge, however, the first of which is the degree to which plant capacity was modernized under the Nazis. West Germany emerged from the war with an enhanced competitive advantage in the production of the high value added consumer goods that were to provide the basis of its post-war export boom. The social-market economy enhanced this by developing institutions which secured the endogenous formation of the skills necessary for technological innovation. Investment in human capital formation and its protection from market penetration generated a permanent supply of valorized labour. This, it was argued in chapter three, was decisive in the capacity of Germany to sustain its industrial dominance. Poland, however, was technologically dependent. The Gierek reforms were based on importing obsolete technology at above market rates. Throughout the 1970s domestic technologies were rejected, traditional production methods rationalized and local enterprises liquidated. Unlike sixteenth-century Poland, during which foreign craftsmen were encouraged to settle, in the 1970s the technology was imported without any instructions for use.[58] The apprenticeship system was abolished and while enterprises did retain extensive on-the-job training, this was progressively diminished during each of the economic reforms as firms were forced to reduce non-productive investment.[59] The second major difference lay in the scale of debt to international institutions. In Germany's case this took the form of reparations for genocide and slave labour which did not assume a significant part of their GNP.[60]

---

58. Tittenbrun, pp. 66–70.
59. World Bank, p. 91. Also OECD, pp. 64–6.
60. See Wolf, 'The Lucky Miracle', pp. 32–3.

In Poland's case by 1989 its debt was $41.4 billion and its interest payments exceeded the amount of credit it had originally received.[61]

The third difference lies in the change in the international consensus effected by the ascendancy of the New Right. Although Germany was militarily defeated and occupied it had a greater degree of autonomy in its choice of institutions than Poland in 1989.[62] The difference in the international consensus between 1945 and 1989 can be gauged from the position of the Catholic Church and labour movement. In West Germany in 1945, trade unions were recognized, particularly in the British zone, as necessary agents in a democratic transformation and the Church supplied one of the primary traditions within which the practices of society were reformed and justified. By 1989, however, trade unions were defined as impediments to reform and the ethical teachings of the Pope on economic justice placed the Church outside the acceptable parameters of political and economic discourse. The conflation of Catholicism and communism is central to Frances Fukayama's explanation of the events of 1989.

> Why was it that these countries moved away from central planning only in the 1980s? The answer must be found in the consciousness of the elites and leaders ruling them, who decided to opt for the 'Protestant' life of wealth and risk over the 'Catholic' path of poverty and security. The change was in no way made inevitable by the material conditions in which either country found itself on the eve of reform, but instead came about as the result of the victory of one idea over another.[63]

To argue that given the choice between the values of Bolshevism and the Catholic labour movement the country chose Protestantism is at best obscure. It does, however, contain two significant insights, namely the possibility of a different response to the task of transformation and the role of ideology in defining reality.

---

61. Tittenbrun, p. 66.

62. This extended to the method of achieving fiscal stability. The IMF played no role in German monetary reform as the deutschmark was not made convertible until 1958. In the Balcerowicz reform 14 per cent of prices were exempt from liberalization in contrast to Erhard's reforms in which the majority of prices remained under control. See Hansonn, 'The 1948 West-German Economic Reforms'.

63. Frances Fukayama, *The End of History and the Last Man,* New York 1992, pp. 64–5.

Market Leninism

In searching for the appropriate conceptual description of the transformation in Poland, the term 'market Leninism' has been adopted as it indicates not only a continuity of policy with the previous regime, but also of method. Leninism assumes uncontested managerial prerogative and the expulsion of institutionalized ethical and social constraints from the domain of economic calculation. Market Leninism is a utopia which shares with its Bolshevik counterpart the elimination of society and its replacement by a managerial vanguard guided by correct theory.[64] Both work with a theory in which exogenous institutions, particularly trade-unions, distort economic calculation leading to mistakes about real interests.[65] Leninism succeeded in hollowing out society with greater thoroughness than the post-war regimes of Western Europe which placed institutional constraints upon economic rationality. Throughout the sphere of Soviet dominion, reciprocity, self-government and inherited forms of practical knowledge withered. Environmental concerns were disregarded, as was safety at work. The enforcement of managerial prerogative was imposed at the expense of vocational, municipal and academic institutions which could have stored and disseminated good economic practice. This method of economic management was continued in the economic reforms initiated after 1989.

An example of this is the plan proposed by Lipton and Sachs which provided the 'blueprint' for the Balcerowicz strategy adopted by the Polish government.[66] The key concept in this new system of social order is 'corporate governance', in which managers play a constitutive role at a non-negotiable

---

64. Wolin wrote that Lenin's conception of vanguard management 'was not merely a quirk of revolutionary theory; . . . it was symptomatic of a broad tendency in twentieth-century thought'. Sheldon S. Wolin, *Politics and Vision*, New York 1960, p. 406.

65. For an account of ultimate subordination of the Soviets to the demands of party management see Samuel Farber, *Before Stalinism: The Rise and Fall of Soviet Democracy*, Cambridge 1990, pp. 19–89, also pp. 188–99.

66. David Lipton and Jeffrey Sachs, 'Privatization in Eastern Europe: The case of Poland', *Brookings Papers on Economic Activity*, Washington DC 1990. Jeffrey Sachs was previously economic advisor to the government of Bolivia and, from the beginning of 1989, Yugoslavia, from whence he was transferred to Poland. See Gowan, p. 7.

institutional level.[67] Sachs claims that his proposals are 'revolutionary without being utopian'.[68] The anti-utopianism derives from the 'relentlessly pragmatic nature' of the goals pursued, defined as 'a recovery of human freedom and a democratically based rise in living standards'.[69] The revolutionary component is the dissolution of existing societal structures by means of state centralization.[70]

In this conception of 'transition' there were two principal forces opposing the privatization process. The first were the nomenklatura 'who appropriate state property by making sweetheart deals with an outside partner', and the second were the works councils established by the Gdansk Accord of 1981.[71] An environment in which 'management were running scared of workers' was contrary to the incentive structures that had to be cultivated in order to establish a 'democratically based rise in living standards'.[72] The means of eliminating both was to nationalize Polish industry, thus defining the property rights in industry as belonging exclusively to the state. Sachs proposed that the 500 largest companies should be 'corporatized' and converted into joint-stock companies with all shares belonging to the Finance Ministry.[73] This would allow the government to 'subcontract the management oversight to an international management consultancy firm' who would enjoy buy-out options after a four year period.[74] These managers thus act as a 'critical mass' on each committee.[75] The justification for nationalization is that: 'A corporate board of directors will be more competent and less subject to political pressures than the government in guiding the process of reconstruction.'[76] As the managers have no contact with the

67. In contrast with post-war West Germany, managers replace organized labour as the institutionally protected force in economic reconstruction.
68. Jeffrey Sachs, *Poland's Jump to the Market Economy*, London 1994, p. 13.
69. Jeffrey Sachs, *Understanding Shock Therapy*, London 1994, p. 25.
70. Sachs, *Jump*, p. 30.
71. Lipton and Sachs, 'Privatization', p. 306.
72. Sachs, *Jump*, p. 34. This is repeated in Balcerowicz, 1995, pp. 179–80.
73. This exceeded the 400 firms already directly under the control of the Finance Ministry and exempt from the 1981 Act.
74. This was subsequently adopted in the 1991 Privatization Act. See Domanski, p. 93, n. 29.
75. Lipton and Sachs, 'Privatization', pp. 319–23.
76. Lipton and Sachs, 'Privatization', p. 327.

history or culture of the society they are moulding, they can rise above politics and impose the discipline of correct procedure.

Through the abolition of works councils in the Privatization Acts of 1990–91, employees lost any influence on managerial appointment or the organization of the enterprise. The centralization of managerial authority in the state-owned enterprises marked a return to the system of managerial prerogative pertaining before the Gdansk Accord of 1981.[77] Panków provides a detailed account of the techniques utilized in order to exclude the workforce from exercising their legal entitlement to participate in the enterprise. By October 1991 only 10 per cent of enterprises obeyed the law on worker consultation.[78] Fear of unemployment, lack of effective representation and progressive impoverishment, as well as the neglect of statutory participation rights, led to a rapid deterioration of productive relations within the firm.[79] The new practices of industrial relations also denied employees access to knowledge of the financial condition of the enterprise. For the first two years of shock therapy, however, there were relatively few strikes. Beginning in February 1992, this changed. Teachers staged a warning strike against their 'pauperization'.[80] 'Solidarity 80' was founded in resistance to government policy and 470 enterprises staged a warning strike over electricity and gas price rises in March. The basic issues raised in the strikes were the distribution of the burdens of transformation and the ownership of the assets inherited from the old regime.[81] According to a survey of attitudes among employees in privatized firms, there was virtual unanimity of support for privatization. The dominant concern, however, was that this would entail a reversion to previous practices in which workers 'were treated like a thing'.[82] Among the workers surveyed, wages were

---

77. Hausner, p. 13.

78. L. Panków, *Work Institutions in Transformation: The Case of Poland 1990–92*, Warsaw 1994.

79. See Wieslawa Kozek, Michael Federowicz and Witold Morawski, 'Poland', in J. Thirkell, R. Scase and S. Vickerstaff, *Labour Relations and Political Change in Eastern Europe: A Comparative Perspective*, London 1995, pp. 109–36.

80. Kloc, 'Polish Labour', p. 143.

81. See Piotr Marciniak, 'Polish Labour Unions: Can They Find a Way Out', *Telos*, No. 92, 1992, pp. 149–57, p. 151.

82. M. Jarosz and M. Kozak, *Denacjonalizcja przedsiebiorstw: Doswiadczenia i wnioski*, in M. Jarosz, ed., *Prywatyzacja: Szance i zagrozenia*, Warsaw 1993, pp. 107–8.

ranked fourth in their priorities behind firm survival, job security and decent treatment.[83] Employees continued to claim that they were co-owners of the enterprise, citing their acceptance of low wages in order to pay off firm debt as proof of their stake and refused to recognise the legitimacy of the state-appointed supervisory board.[84]

The priority of the formal as opposed to the substantive conception of economics assumed by shock therapy resulted in seven times more aid being directed to the Ministry of Ownership Changes than to the Ministry of Industry and Trade.[85] The Polish Government 'anticipated that foreign investors will provide a large share of the capital, technology, and general managerial know-how necessary to support the transformation of state-owned enterprises into privately owned, efficient firms'.[86] Laws were passed in 1991 which enabled foreign-owned companies to transfer all their profits out of the country and exempted them from licensing laws. The total amount of investment by June 1991, however, was only $580 million.[87] Just as in the Gierek reforms, Western management techniques and technology were assumed to bring economic benefits while the result was an intensification of debt, fiscal crisis and a further reduction of high value added manufacture. Whereas Erhard failed in his attempt to restore the Weimar Commercial Code in 1947, which would have made co-determination illegal, the 1934 Commercial Code was restored in Poland rendering enterprise democracy unconstitutional.[88] The Polish Alliance of Crafts, which functioned before 1939 as a national Handwerk organisation, reformed after 1989 and

---

83. See J. Gardawski and T. Zukowski, *Politika i gospodarka w oczach pracownikow*, Warsaw 1992.

84. Chelminski, 'New Forms of State Ownership', p. 193.

85. OECD, p. 86. Western 'technical assistance' took the form of subsidizing consulting agencies which evaluated Polish companies and passed the information on to their Western clients. See Janine R. Wedel, 'The Unintended Consequences of Western Aid to Post-Communist Europe', *Telos*, No. 92, 1992, pp. 131–8. For an analysis of how 'aid' led to the transfer of information from east to west, as well as the non-payment of much of the Phare programme funded by the EU, see Gowan, pp. 35–8.

86. OECD, p. 40.

87. This is less than the net worth of footballers playing in the top ten English Premier league teams in the season 1995–6.

88. See chapter three, pp. 64–9.

requested a restoration of self-government in the granting of licences. This was refused by the new administration on the grounds of economic efficiency.[89]

Polanyi's argument developed in chapter one was that in a market 'storm' societal resistance would cluster around human beings and nature and oppose their transformation into the commodity fictions of labour and land. After 1989 the elements of Polish culture were besieged. The ex-Communists and Peasants' Party have become dominant because they argue that the state can slow down the rate of change through easing market pressures on labour, land and the productive organizations of society.[90] They are playing the role of the Tudor monarchy in sixteenth-century England, the German aristocracy in the eighteenth century and the peasant parties, Church and nobility throughout central Europe in the nineteenth century.[91]

In 1981 Solidarity redefined liberal democracy through the idea of the self-governing republic. The subsequent subordination of democracy to the demands of fiscal correctness, the collapse of liberalism into deregulation and the affirmation of self-interest as the principal source of social renewal have characterized the present transformation. In *The Class Struggles in France*, Marx writes that:

> After the revolution, when the liberal banker Laffitte led his companion the Duke of Orleans in triumph to the Hotel de Ville, he let fall the words, 'from now on the bankers will rule.' Laffitte had betrayed the revolution.[92]

The deepest irony of the present transformation is that it furnishes an empirical vindication of Marx's theory.

---

89. Hausner, p. 44. Between 1989 and 1992, half a per cent of the population were involved in training, and spending on labour market policies accounted for 0.22 per cent of budget expenditure. World Bank, p. xii.

90. The parliamentary elections of 1993 initiated a policy of restructuring, rather than eliminating industry.

91. See chapter one, pp. 5–19. TGT, p. 183.

92. Karl Marx, *Selected Writings*, ed. David McLellan, Oxford 1977, p. 286.

Conclusion

This book has told a story of an event that did not happen. In order to establish its force, it was essential that the non-event in question, the implementation of the Solidarity programme following their electoral victory in 1989, was a viable alternative. To establish this, it was argued that the West German economy, because of its labour market restrictions, democratic interferences, structure of solidarity and apprenticeship systems, is the most consistently productive economy in Europe. It remained so by assimilating technological innovations within its traditional institutions of knowledge and status. It was both an economically efficient model and an example of how a society could be institutionally re-formed after a period of dictatorship. In order to establish that this form of social organization was possible in Poland, there had to be the cultural and institutional possibilities within the country that could provide the agency and language necessary to construct such an order. The ideas developed by Solidarity in 1981 and repeated in the 1989 *Position* document show that such ideas were not so much present, as dominant. The institutional legacy was the factory councils established after the signing of the Gdansk Accord. 'Christian ethics and the democratic traditions of the labour world' provided the ideological basis of opposition.[1]

It also had to be established that there was an economic, political and ideological sphere that could provide the recognition, resources and practices necessary to effect insertion within the international political and economic system. From its creation the

---

1. See Solidarity, p. 327.

EU was based on protectionism for peasants and workers in the form of pig iron quotas and pig farm subsidies. The European Union, however, was a political and economic but not an ideological presence. The breakdown in the post-war consensus had rendered its practices inadmissible.

The European post-war settlement had rested upon four institutions. The first was the balance of power of the Cold War. This divided the richer from the poorer parts of the continent, externalized a large part of the military cost, while effectively inhibiting any exchange between East and West. The second was the Bretton Woods system which protected domestic purchasing power by resisting currency speculation. The opinion of the financial markets was offset by the combined assets of each major industrial nation. The chimera of the gold standard may have evaporated but its phantom lived on in the Federal Reserve Bank.[2] The consequence of its collapse has been an ever-dwindling opportunity to pursue an autonomous national industrial or welfare policy through the sanction of capital flight and currency collapse.[3] This has led to unrelenting pressure on the third element, the welfare state, as the guarantor of the necessities of life. The financial crisis of the welfare state was the domestic centrepiece of the New Right agenda. The fourth element of the post-war settlement was that of the mixed economy which is in the advanced stage of privatization.

Nazism was understood as a result of the great depression, and the elimination of the conditions of Fascist renewal, most particularly high unemployment, was a conscious goal of post-war reconstruction.[4] Its defining feature was that labour and land were protected from unmediated dependence on the price system. Medical services, education, house building, agricultural production and employment were all either directly administered by the state, regulated or maintained through transfer payments. The distinction between necessary and unnecessary suffering, it was argued, defines the scope of politics to ameliorate the miseries of life.[5] Suffering is necessary but it need not be relentless. The post-

---

2. Arrighi, p. 278.

3. This was the 'lesson' of the Mitterrand 'experiment'. See chapter five.

4. The international consensus was built around the successes of the New Deal in stabilizing society, reflating the economy and mobilizing political support in the United States during the 1930s. See Charles S. Maier, 'The Politics of Productivity'.

5. TGT, p. 255.

war settlement provided a degree of security against destitution and a level of solidarity that increased freedom while lessening exploitation. Both economic liberalism and statist communitarianism were defined as utopian and unsustainable principles of social order and were subordinated to the autonomy of the person and the societal institutions which recognize their status as beings capable of trust, conscience and skill.

Within the 'European Economic Space' envisaged by Walter Funk, the German economic minister in 1940, Germany was to be the centre of European manufacture, its currency would dominate exchange within the continent and its welfare levels would remain higher than the elaborately ranked societies that participated in the New Economic Order.[6] This was not, however, achieved militarily. The most democratic economy in Europe underpins continental fiscal stability. The priority of society proved more effective than the apotheosis of the state.

Germany transformed its collective identity after 1945 through the establishment of unique labour-market and welfare institutions. These societal innovations were combined with a political constitution based on the priority of individual rights. While every major state in Western Europe developed a strong central bank, extended welfare rights and adopted an industrial policy after 1945, the degree of democracy and status protection established within German society was greater than in any other country participating in the world economy. The restoration of societal institutions with a direct function in the economy did not trail along in the wake of central bank policy and Marshall Aid after 1948. Not financial policy but industrial practice was the motor of societal restoration, and this demanded new institutional arrangements within the labour market. Co-determination, Handwerk production, vocational training and the self-organization of pension funds were the institutional means developed in the Federal Republic through which a democratic society could re-form itself after Nazism. West Germany succeeded in institutionalizing constraints on managerial prerogative in the organization of the labour process. The result was a degree of productive innovation

---

6. See C.W. Guillebaud, 'Hitler's New Economic order for Germany', *Economic Journal*, Vol. 50, 1940, pp. 449–60. For an extensive account of Funk's conception of the European Economic Space see Keith Tribe, 'The New Economic Order and European Economic Integration', *Strategies of Economic Order*, pp. 241–62.

and political stability unprecedented in German, or European, history. That era has come to an end. With unification a national and not a social logic has characterized German policy. Workers' rights have been overruled and co-determination has no status in international law. The integration of East Germany has been based on the imposition and not the negotiation of common rules.

Jürgen Habermas poses an opposition between a life world and a systems world. The former is characterized by undominated communication and the latter by the imperatives of rational calculation and bureaucratic administration.[7] This has not been the approach developed here. The distinction advanced is between managerial authority and the practical activity of labour; the forces and relations of knowledge. Under real existing socialism, the practices of production were subordinated to the imperatives of administration, in the state, the firm and the educational system. Employees were compensated outside the world of work with a range of welfare guarantees. Within the enterprise, however, the authority of management was consistently upheld. Any compromise was acceptable other than employee participation in the management of the firm. This imperative method has been consolidated by the type of economic reform since adopted after 1989.

A market economy, Polanyi argues, requires a non-market society in order to renew its technologies of survival. Non-contractual organizations which teach and preserve skills, and cultivate a conception of the person capable of responsible co-operation on the basis of their acquired knowledge, while providing for human needs outside the price system, are necessary features of societies which adopt market principles of international competition. A competitive market for commodities does not require factor markets in labour and land. During the transformation in Poland after 1989, however, the formal definition of economic rationality has been imposed on society, thus emptying it of its substantive content.

A consensus plays a central role in allocating the burdens of association, for it defines the capacity of society to respond to the miseries of life. The power of a consensus lies in its ability to define alternatives as insane. The Parisian craftsmen of 1848 were

---

7. See Jürgen Habermas, 'Labour and Interaction: Remarks on Hegel's Jena "Philosophy of Spirit"', in *Theory and Practice*, Cambridge 1989. For a more general discussion see *A Theory of Communicative Action: Vol. 2*, Cambridge 1987.

excluded from intellectual respectability by each of the competing ideologies, as was the early Labour Party.[8] The workers in Germany in 1918 were regarded as a threat to democracy in their demands for 'decent human treatment' by the alliance of forces which provided support for the Nazi take-over of power fifteen years later.[9] The Solidarity movement has been liquidated by market forces.[10] The three demands of human survival that each of these defeated movements upheld have not disappeared through methodological avoidance. The necessity of work in a material, cultural and ethical sense, the embedded nature of economic activity and the non-commodity status of human beings and nature remain relevant despite academic neglect. The idea that the self-organized institutions of society could democratically organize the satisfaction of needs and the preservation of culture by subordinating both the state and market to the demands of a decentralized democracy provided the ideological foundation for the practices of labour relations, subsidiarity and federalism characteristic of West Germany after 1948. It was also the ideal around which Polish Solidarity clustered in 1981 through their idea of a self-governing republic. It has been argued in this book that the uneasy sovereignty of state and market, the dialectic of starvation and war, have only been restrained by strengthening the principles characteristic of 1848 in Paris, 1948 in Hesse and 1981 in Gdansk. The conclusion presented here is that socialism is a precondition of viable capitalism.

---

8. See chapter two.
9. See chapter three.
10. See chapter six.

Bibliography

Abel, W., *Massenarmut und Hungerkrisen im vorindustriellen Deutschland*, Göttingen 1972.

Abelshauser, W., *Wirtschaft in Westdeutschland 1945–1948. Rekonstruktion und Wachstumsbedingungen in der amerikanischen und britischen Zone*, Stuttgart 1975.

Abelshauser, W., 'The Economic Policy of Ludwig Erhard', EUI Working Paper, Florence 1984, p. 11.

Adam, J., 'The Transition to a Market Economy in Poland', *Cambridge Journal of Economics*, Vol. 18, 1994, pp. 607–18.

Anderson, M., 'Piety and Politics: Recent Work on German Catholicism', *Journal of Modern History*, Vol. 63, 1991, pp. 681–786.

Aoki, M., 'Horizontal Versus Vertical Information Structure of the Firm', *American Economic Review*, Vol. 76, 1986, pp. 971–83.

Arrighi, G., *The Long Twentieth Century: Money, Power and the Origins of Our Times*, London 1995.

Balcerowicz, L., *Socialism, Capitalism and Transformation*, Budapest 1995.

Beissinger, M., *Scientific Management, Socialist Discipline and Soviet Power*, Cambridge Mass. 1988.

Berenson, F., *Populist Religion and Left-Wing Politics in France 1830–52*, New Jersey 1982.

Bergahn, V., *The Americanisation of German Industry 1945–1973*, New York 1986.

Bernhard, M.H., 'The Strikes of June 1976 in Poland', *East European Politics and Societies*, Vol. 1, No. 3, 1987, pp. 363–92.

Bernhard, M.H., *The Origins of Democratization in Poland:*

Workers, Intellectuals and Oppositional Politics, 1976–1980, New York 1993.

Bernstein, E., *Die Voraussetzungen des Sozialismus und die Aufgaben der Sozialdemokratie*, Stuttgart 1920.

Bessel, R., 'Unemployment and Demobilisation in Germany after the First World War', in R.J. Evans and R. Geary, eds, *The German Unemployed: Experiences and Consequences of Mass Unemployment from the Weimar Republic to the Third Reich*, London 1987, pp. 23–43.

Bessel, R., *Germany After the First World War*, Oxford 1993.

Beveridge, W., *Social Insurance and Allied Benefits*, London 1942.

Biernacki, R., *The Fabrication of Labour, Germany and Britain: 1640–1914*, California 1995.

Blackbourn, D., *Class, Religion and Local Politics in Wilhelmine Germany: The Centre Party in Württemberg before 1914*, New Jersey 1989.

Blanc, L., 'The Organisation of Labour', in A. Fried and R. Sanders, eds, *Socialist Thought, A Documentary History*, New York 1992, pp. 231–7.

Boswell, J., *Community and the Economy: The Theory of Public Co-operation*, London 1990.

Bowen, R.H., *German Theories of the Corporate State: With Special Reference to the Period 1870–1914*, New York 1947.

Bowles, S., Gordon, D., and Weisskopf, T., 'Power, Accumulation and Crisis: The Rise and Demise of the Post-war Social Structure of Accumulation', in S. Bowles and R. Edwards, eds, *Radical Political Economy*, Vol. 2, Aldershot 1990.

Bowles, S. and Gintis, G., 'A Political and Economic Case For The Democratic Enterprise', *Economics and Philosophy*, Vol. 9, 1993, pp. 75–100.

Briefs, G., *The Proletariat*, New York 1937.

Brock, P., 'The Socialists of the Polish Great Immigration' in A. Briggs and J. Saville, eds, *Essays in Labour History*, London 1967, pp. 140–73.

Brusco S. and Sabel, C. F., 'Artisanal Production and Economic Growth', in F. Wilkinson, ed., *The Dynamics of Labour Market Segmentation*, London 1981, pp. 99–114.

Brusco, S., 'The Emilian Model: Productive Decentralisation and Social Integration', *Cambridge Journal of Economics*, Vol. 6, No. 2, 1982. pp. 167–84.

Bunn, R.F., 'The Ideology of the Federation of German Employers'

Associations', *American Journal of Economics and Sociology*, Vol. 18, No. 4, 1959, pp. 369–79.

Bunn, R.F., 'The Federation of German Employers' Associations: A Political Interest Group', *Western Political Quarterly*, Vol. 13, No. 3, 1960, pp. 652–69.

Camp, R., *The Papal Ideology of Social Reform: A Study in Historical Development*, Leiden 1969.

Campbell, J.L., 'The Fiscal Crisis of Post-Communist States', *Telos*, No. 93, 1992, pp. 89–110.

Carlin, W., 'Economic Reconstruction in West-Germany: 1945–55: The Displacement of "Vegetative Controls"', in I.D. Turner, ed., *Reconstruction in Post-War Germany: British Occupation Policy and the Western Zones 1945–55*, Oxford 1989, pp. 37–65.

Casey, B., 'The Dual Apprenticeship System and the Recruitment and Retention of Young Persons in West-Germany', *British Journal of Industrial Relations*, Vol. 24, No. 4, 1986, pp. 63–81.

Chase, M., *'The People's Farm': English Radical Agrarianism 1775–1840*, Oxford 1988.

Chelminski, D., Czynzyk, A.A., and Sterniczuk, H., 'New Forms of State Ownership in Poland: The Case of Commercialization', in G.S. Alexander and G. Skapska, eds, *A Fourth Way? Privatization, Property and the Emergence of New Market Economies*, London 1994, pp. 182–97.

Ciechocinska, M., *Polozenie klasy robotniczej w Polsce 1929–1939*, Warsaw 1965.

Claeys, G., *Machinery, Money and the Millennium: From Moral Economy to Socialism*, Cambridge 1987.

Cohen, G.A., 'The Structure of Proletarian Unfreedom', *Philosophy and Public Affairs*, Vol. 13, No. 1, 1982.

Cole, G.D.H., *The History of Socialist Thought, Vol. 1: The Forerunners, 1789–1850*, London 1953.

Connor, I , 'The Churches and the Refugee Problem in Bavaria 1945–1949', *Journal of Contemporary History*, Vol. 20, 1985, pp. 399–421.

Crouch, C., 'Co-operation and Competition in an Institutionalised Economy: The Case of Germany', in C. Crouch and D. Marquand, eds, *Ethics and Markets: Co-operation and Competition Within Capitalist Economies*, Oxford 1993, pp. 80–98.

Crozier, M.J., Huntington, S.P. and Watanuki, J., *The Crisis of*

Democracy: Report on the Governability of Democracies to the Trilateral Commission, New York 1975.

Daniel, K., 'Private Ownership in a Changing Poland: Myth and Reality', in G.S. Alexander and G. Skapska, eds, *A Fourth Way? Privatisation, Property and the Emergence of New Market Economies*, London 1994, pp. 138–49.

Dartmann, C., 'Redistribution of Power, Joint Consultation or Productivity Coalition? Labour and Post-War reconstruction in Germany and Britain, 1945–1953', Bochum 1996.

D'Entreves, A.P., ed., *Aquinas*, Oxford 1978.

Derry, T.K., 'The Repeal of the Apprenticeship Clauses of the Statutes of Apprenticeship', *Economic History Review*, Vol. 3, 1931, pp. 67–87.

Dierickx, G., 'Christian Democracy and Its Ideological Rivals', in David Hanley, ed., *Christian Democracy in Europe: A Comparative Perspective*, London 1994, pp. 15–30.

Ditt, K. and Kift, D., eds, *1889: Bergarbeiterstreik und Wilhelminische Gesellschaft*, Hagan 1989.

Dobson, C.R., *Masters and Journeymen: A Prehistory of Industrial Relations 1717–1800*, London 1980.

Domanski, S.R., 'The Quest for Ownership. Why it was so easy to break communism, and why it is so difficult to find social consensus: A response to the "Surprise Literature"', *Eastern European Economics*, Vol. 32, No. 2, 1994, pp. 71–94.

Donzelot, J., 'The Promotion of the Social', *Economy and Society*, Vol. 17, No. 3, 1988, pp. 395–427.

Doran, A., *Craft Enterprises in Britain and Germany: A Sectoral Study*, London 1984.

Dorr, D., *Options for the Poor: A Hundred Years of Vatican Social Teaching*, Dublin 1983.

Dosi, G., 'Sources, Procedures and Microeconomic Effects of Innovation', *Journal of Economic Literature*, Vol. 26, 1988, pp. 1120–71.

Durkheim, E., *Professional Ethics and Civic Morals*, London 1992.

Duroselle, J.B., *Les débuts du Catholique Social en France (1822–1870)*, Paris 1951.

Dürr, E.W.F., *Ordoliberalismus und Sozialpolitik*, Winterthur 1954.

Dziecielska-Machnikowskka, S. and Matuszak G., *Czternascie lodzkich miesiecy*, Lodz 1984.

Eisenberg, C., 'Working-Class Politics and the Cold War: American Intervention in the German Labour Movement, 1945–1949', *Diplomatic History*, Vol. 7, No. 4, 1983, pp. 283–306.

Elam, M., 'Markets, Morals and the Powers of Innovation', *Economy and Society*, Vol. 22, No. 1, 1993, pp. 1–41.

Eucken, W., 'Die Wettbewerbsordnung und ihre Verwirklichung', in *ORDO – Jahrbuch für die Ordnung von Wirtschaft und Gesellschaft*, Vol. 2, 1949, pp. 381–98.

Farber, S., *Before Stalinism: The Rise and Fall of Soviet Democracy*, Cambridge 1990.

Farquharson, J.E., *The Western Allies and the Politics of Food: Agricultural Management in Post-War Germany*, New Hampshire 1985.

Feiwel, G., 'Pressures, Breakdown and Optimism in Planning' in *Industrialisation and Planning Under Polish Socialism*, New York 1971, pp. 261–78.

Fellanbuchl, Z., 'The Polish Economy in the 1970s', *East European Economies Post-Helsinki*, Washington DC 1977, pp 832–4.

Festinger, L., *A Theory of Cognitive Dissonance*, Chicago 1957.

Fischer, M.J., *Iran: From Religious Dispute to Revolution*, Cambridge Mass. 1980.

Fischer, W., *Handwerksrecht und Handwerkswirtschaft um 1800: Studien zur Sozial- und Wirtschaftsverfassung vor der industriellen Revolution*, Berlin 1955.

Flakierski, H., 'The Polish Economic Reforms' in Simon McInness (ed.), *The Soviet Union and East Europe into the 1980s*, Ontario 1976, pp. 175–203.

Fones-Wolf, E., *Selling Free Enterprise*, Illinois 1995.

Forest, A., *The French Revolution and the Poor*, London 1981.

Franz, W. and Soskice, D., 'The German Apprenticeship System', Working Paper FSO 94-302, Wissenschaftszentrum Berlin für Sozialforschung, Berlin 1994.

Frieden, J.A., *Banking on the World: The Politics of American International Finance*, New York 1987.

Friedman, M. and Schwartz, A.J., *A Monetary History of the United States 1867–1960*, New Jersey 1963.

Friedman, M., 'The Counter Revolution in Monetary Theory', Paper 33, IEA, London 1970.

Gardawski, J. and Zukowski, T., *Politika i gospodarka w oczach pracownikow*, Warsaw 1992.

Gaye, M., *What's Going On?*, Detroit 1972.

Georges, D., *Handwerk und Interessenpolitik: Von der Zunft zur modernen Verbandsorganisation*, Frankfurt 1993.

Gewirth, A., *The Principle Of Generative Consistency*, Chicago 1977, p. 14.

Giersch, H., Paqué, H.H. and Schmeidling, H., *The Fading Miracle: Four Decades of Market Economy in Germany*, Cambridge 1993.

Gillingham, J.R., 'Industrial Apprenticeships and "Deproletarianisation": Labour Training in the Third Reich', *Central European History*, Vol. 18, 1985.

Gillingham, J.R., *Industry and Politics in the Third Reich: Ruhr Coal, Hitler and Europe*, New York 1985.

Gimbel, J., *The American Occupation of Germany: Politics and the Military 1945–49*, Stanford 1968.

Gladen, A., 'Die Streiks der Bergarbeiter im Ruhrgebiet in den Jahren 1889, 1905 und 1912', in J. Rulecke, ed., *Arbeiterbewegung an Rhein und Ruhr: Beiträge zur Geschichte der Arbeiterbewegung in Rheinland-Westfalen*, Wuppertal 1974, pp. 111–48.

Glees, A., *Exile Politics During the Second World War: The Social Democrats in Britain*, Oxford 1982.

Goodway, D., *London Chartism 1838–1848*, Cambridge 1982.

Gordon, D., 'The Global Economy: New Edifice or Crumbling Foundations', *New Left Review*, No. 168, 1988, pp. 24–65.

Gowan, P., 'Neo-Liberal Theory and Practice for Eastern Europe', *New Left Review*, No. 213, 1995, pp. 3–60.

Green, P., 'The Third Round in Poland', *New Left Review*, No. 101–2, 1977, pp. 69–108.

Guillebaud, C.W., *The Works Councils: A German Experiment in Industrial Democracy*, Cambridge 1928.

Guillebaud, C.W., 'Hitler's New Economic Order for Germany', *Economic Journal*, Vol. 50, 1940, pp. 449–60.

Habermas, J., *A Theory of Communicative Action: Vol. 2*, Cambridge 1987.

Habermas, J., 'Labour and Interaction: Remarks on Hegel's Jena "Philosophy of Spirit"' in *Theory and Practice*, Cambridge 1989.

Hahn, C.M., 'Radical Functionalism: The Life and Work of Karl Polanyi', *Dialectical Anthropology*, Vol. 17, 1992, pp. 141–66.

Hampshire-Monk, I., 'John Thelwall and the Eighteenth Century Response to Political Economy', *Historical Journal*, Vol. 45, 1991, pp. 1–20.

Hansonn, A.H., 'The 1948 West-German Economic Reforms: A Model for Eastern Europe?', Working Paper of the University of British Columbia No. 90-05, Vancouver 1990.

Harhoff, D. and Kane, T.J., 'Financing Apprenticeship Training: The Evidence from Germany', Working Paper of the National Bureau of Economic Research No. 4557, Massachusetts 1993.

Harman, C., *Class Struggles in Eastern Europe 1945–1983*, London 1988.

Harvey, A., 'Four Pieces of the Unemployment Puzzle', manuscript presented at the Royal Economics Society, Southampton 1995.

Hausner, J., *Populist Threat in Transformation of Socialist Society*, Warsaw 1992.

Hayek, F.A., *The Three Sources of Human Values*, London 1978.

Hayek, F.A., *Law Legislation and Liberty Vol. 1: Rules and Order*, London 1973.

Hayek, F.A., *Law, Legislation and Liberty Vol. 2: The Mirage of Social Justice*, London 1976.

Hayek, F.A., *Law, Legislation and Liberty, Vol. 3: The Political Order of a Free People*, London 1979.

Hayek, F.A., *Knowledge, Evolution and Society*, London 1983.

Hayek, F.A., *The Fatal Conceit: The Errors of Socialism*, London 1988.

Hayek, F.A., *Economic Freedom*, London 1991.

Hegel, G.W.F., *Elements of the Philosophy of Right*, ed. Allen W. Wood, Cambridge 1991.

Hegel, G.W.F. *Jenenser Realphilosophie*, Vol. 2, ed. J. Hoffmeister, Leipzig 1931.

Heller, W.W., 'The Role of Fiscal Monetary Policy in the German Economic Recovery', *American Economic Review*, Vol. 40, No. 2, 1950.

Heschel, S., 'Nazifying Christian Theology: Walter Grundmann and the Institute for the Study and Eradication of Jewish Influence on German Church Life', *Church History*, Vol. 63, No. 4, 1994.

Hill, C., *Reformation to Industrial Revolution: A Social and Economic History of Britain, 1530–1780*, London 1967.

Hirst, P. and Zeitlin, J., 'Flexible Specialisation versus Post-

Fordism: Theory, Evidence and Policy Implications', *Economy and Society*, Vol. 20, No. 1, 1991, pp. 1–56.

Hockerts, H.G., 'German Post-War Social Policies Against the Background of the Beveridge Plan', in W.J. Mommsen, ed., *The Emergence of the Welfare State in Britain and Germany*, London 1981, pp. 315–39.

Hogan, W.E., *The Development of Bishop Wilhelm Emmanuel Von Ketteler's Interpretation of the Social Problem*, Washington DC 1946.

Hussain, A. and Tribe, K., *Marxism and the Agrarian Question*, London 1983.

Jarosz, M. and Kozak, M., *Denacjonalizcja przedsiebiorstw: Doswiadczenia i wnioski*, in M. Jarosz, ed., *Prywatyzacja: Szance i zagrozenia*, Warsaw 1993.

Jarosz, M., ed., *Employee-Owned Companies in Poland*, Warsaw 1994.

John-Paul II, 'Laborem Exercens: On Human Work' (1981) in O'Brien and Shannon, eds, *Catholic Social Thought*, pp. 352–92.

John-Paul II, 'Centesimus Annus: On the Hundredth Anniversary of *Rerum Novarum*' (1991) in O'Brien and Shannon, *Catholic Social Thought*, pp. 439–88.

John, P., *Handwerk im Spannungsfeld zwischen Zunftordnung und Gewerbefreiheit*, Cologne 1987.

Kant, I., 'The Metaphysics of Morals', in H. Riess, ed., *Kant: Political Writings*, Cambridge 1991, pp. 132–75.

Kant, I., *Religion Within the Limits of Reason Alone*, New York 1960.

Katter, M.H., *The Nazi Party, A Social Profile of Members and Leaders 1919–1945*, Cambridge 1983.

Kaufmann, F.X., 'The Churches and the Emergent Welfare State in Germany', *ISB Materialien No. 11*, Institut für Bevölkerungsforschung und Sozialpolitik, Bielefeld 1983.

Keller, B., *Das Handwerk im faschistischen Deutschland*, Cologne 1980.

Kellett, J.R., 'The Breakdown of Gild and Corporation Control over the Handicraft and Retail Trade of London', *Economic History Review*, Vol. 10, No. 3, 1958.

Ketteler, W.E. von, *Die Arbeitfrage und Das Christenthum*, Mainz 1864.

Keynes, J.M., *A Treatise on Money*, Vol. 2, London 1930.

Kloc, K., 'Polish Labour in Transition: 1990–1992', *Telos*, No. 92, 1992, pp. 139–48.

Koch, M.J., *Die Bergarbeiterbewegung im Ruhrgebiet zur Zeit Wilhelms II, 1889–1914*, Düsseldorf 1954.

Kocka, J., 'The First World War and the *Mittelstand*: German Artisans and White Collar Workers', *Journal of Contemporary History*, No. 8, 1973, pp. 100–23.

Kocka, J., *Facing Total War: German Society 1914–1918*, Leamington Spa 1984.

Kolodko G. and Gotz-Kozierkiewicz, D., 'Fiscal Adjustment and Stabilization Policies in Eastern Europe', *Oxford Review of Economic Policy*, Vol. 8, No. 1, 1993.

Kostrewski, J., 'Na smierc rad rebotniczych', *Biuletyn Informacyjny 26*, 1978, pp. 16–20.

Kowalik, T., 'Reply to Maurice Glasman', *New Left Review*, No. 206, 1994, p. 138.

Kowalik, T., 'The Free Market or a Social Contract as Bases of Systemic Transformation', in J. Hausner, B. Jessop and K. Nielson, eds, *Strategic Choice and Path-Dependency in Post-Socialism: Institutional Dynamics in the Transformation Process*, Aldershot 1995, pp. 131–48.

Kozek, W., Federowicz, M. and Morawski, W., 'Poland', in J. Thirkell, R. Scase and S. Vickerstaff, eds, *Labour Relations and Political Change in Eastern Europe: A Comparative Perspective*, London 1995, pp. 109–36.

Kuhn, T.S., *The Structure of Scientific Revolutions*, 2nd edn, Chicago 1970.

Laba, R., *The Roots of Solidarity: A Political Sociology of Poland's Working Class Democratization*, Princeton 1991.

Lakatos, I., 'Falsification and the Methodology of Scientific Research Programmes', in I. Lakatos and A. Musgrave, eds, *Criticism and the Growth of Knowledge*, Cambridge 1970, pp. 91–196.

Lakatos, I., 'History of Science and Rational Reconstructions', in R.C. Buch and R.S. Cohen, eds, *Boston Studies in the Philosophy of Science*, Vol. 8, Dortrecht 1974.

Lane, C., 'Industrial Change in Europe: The Pursuit of Flexible Specialisation in Britain and West-Germany', *Work Employment and Society*, Vol. 12, No. 2, 1988, pp. 141–68.

Lazonik, W., *Competitive Advantage on the Shop Floor*, Cambridge Mass. 1990.

Lenin, V.I., *What is to be Done?*, New York 1902.

Leo XIII, 'Rerum Novarum: The Condition of Labour' (1891) in O'Brien and Shannon, *Catholic Social Thought*, pp. 14–40.

Lipton D. and Sachs, J., 'Privatization in Eastern Europe: The case of Poland', *Brookings Papers on Economic Activity*, Washington DC 1990.

Lockett, R., *Thinking the Unthinkable*, London 1994.

Lombard, M., 'A Re-examination of the Reasons for the Failure of Keynesian Expansionary Policies in France, 1981–1983', *Cambridge Journal of Economics*, Vol. 19, 1995, pp. 359–72.

MacDonald, O., 'The Polish Vortex: Solidarity and Socialism', *New Left Review*, No. 139, 1983, pp. 5–48.

Machiavelli, N., *The Prince*, ed. Q. Skinner and R. Price, Cambridge 1994.

MacIntyre, A., *After Virtue: A Study in Moral Theory*, London 1985.

MacIntyre, A., 'Epistemological Crisis. Dramatic Narrative and the Philosophy of Science', *The Monist*, Vol. 4, 1977, pp. 453–72.

Magraw, R., *A History of the French Working-Class, Vol. 2: The Age of the Artisan Radicals*, Oxford 1992, pp. 147–60.

Mahnkopf, B., 'The "Skill-Oriented" Strategies of German Trade Unions: Their Impact on Efficiency and Equality Objectives', *British Journal of Industrial Relations*, Vol. 30, No. 1, 1992, pp. 61–82.

Maier, C.S., 'The Politics of Productivity: Foundations of American International Policy after World War Two', in P.J. Katzenstein, ed., *Between Power and Plenty: Foreign Economic Policies of Advanced Industrial States*, Wisconsin 1978.

Maier, H., *Revolution and Church: The Early History of Christian Democracy, 1789–1901*, Notre Dame 1969.

Maitland, I., *The Causes of Industrial Disorder: A Comparison of a British and German Factory*, London 1983.

Malthus, T.R., *An Essay on the Principle of Population*, ed. Donald Winch, Cambridge 1992 [1798].

Manderhausen, H., 'Prices, Money and the Distribution of Goods in Post-war Germany' *American Economic Review*, Vol. 39, 1949, pp. 646–72.

Marciniak, P., 'Polish Labour Unions: Can They Find a Way Out', *Telos*, No. 92, 1992, pp. 149–57.

Marshall, T.H., *Citizenship and Social Class*, London 1950.

Marx, K., *Selected Writings*, ed. David McLellan, Oxford 1977.

Marx, K. and Engels, F., *Manifesto of the Communist Party*, London 1996.

Mason, T.D. and Krane, D.A., 'The Political-Economy of the Death Squads: Towards a Theory of the Impact of State Sanctioned Terror', *International Studies Quarterly*, Vol. 33, 1989, pp. 199–231.

Matysiak, T., *Przed Konfliktem – Konflikt*, Warsaw 1986.

Mazor, I., 'The Decay of the Command Economies', *East-European Economy and Society*, Vol. 8, No. 2, 1994.

McKitrick, F.L., 'Old World Craftsmen into Modern Capitalists: Artisans in Germany from National Socialism to the Federal Republic, 1939–1953', Doctoral Dissertation of the Faculty of Arts and Sciences, Columbia University 1994.

McNally, D., *Against the Market: Political Economy, Market Socialism and the Marxist Critique*, London 1993.

Mellor, R.E.H., *The Two Germanies: A Modern Geography*, London 1974.

Messerlin, P.A., 'The Association Agreements between the EC and Central Europe: Trade Liberalism vs Constitutional Failure?', in J. Flemming and J.M.C. Rollo, eds, *Trade, Payments and Adjustment in Central and Eastern Europe*, London 1992.

Mill, J.S., *On Liberty*, London 1984.

Milward, A.S., *The Reconstruction of Western Europe 1945–1951*, Berkeley 1984.

Mizgala, J.J., 'The Ecology of Transformation: The Impact of the Corporate State on the Development of the Party system in Poland, 1989–93', *East European Politics and Society*, Vol. 8, No. 2, 1993, pp. 358–68.

Mommsen, H., *From Weimar to Auschwitz*, Cambridge 1992.

Mommsen, H., 'Class War or Co-determination: On the control of Economic Power in the Weimar Republic', in *From Weimar to Auschwitz*, pp. 62–78.

Mommsen, H., 'State and Bureaucracy in the Brüning Era', in *From Weimar to Auschwitz*, pp. 79–118.

Mommsen, H., '20 July 1944 and the German Labour Movement', in *From Weimar to Auschwitz*, pp. 189–207.

Mommsen, W.J., 'The German Revolution 1918–1920: Political Revolution or Social Protest Movement', in R. Bessel and E.J. Feuchtwanger, eds, *Social Change and Political Development in Weimar Germany*, London 1991, pp. 21–34.

Moore, B. Jr., *Injustice: The Social Bases of Obedience and Revolt*, Cambridge 1978.

Moss, B.H., *The Origins of the French Labour Movement: The Socialism of Skilled Workers 1830–1914*, Berkeley 1976.

Mueller, C., *The Politics of Communication*, Oxford 1973.

Muet, P.A., 'Economic Management and the International Environment 1981–83', in H. Machin and V. Wright, eds, *Economic and Policy Making Under the Mitterrand Presidency 1981–84*, London 1985.

Munoz-Darde, V., *Fraternité, Un concept politique?* Paris 1997.

Murray, C., *Losing Ground*, New York 1984.

Murrell, P., 'What is Shock Therapy? What did it do in Poland and Russia?', *Post-Soviet Affairs*, Vol. 9, No. 2, 1993, pp. 111–40.

Naphtali, F., *Wirtschaftsdemokratie, Ihr Wesen, Weg und Ziel*, Berlin 1928.

Nef, J.U., 'The Progress of Technology and the Growth of Large-Scale Industry in Great Britain, 1560–1640', *Economic History Review*, Vol. 5, No. 1, 1934.

Nicholls, A.J., *Freedom with Responsibility: The Social Market in Germany 1918–1963*, Oxford 1994.

Noyes, P.H., *Organisation and Revolution: Working-Class Associations in the German Revolution of 1848–1849*, Princeton 1966.

Nozick, R., *Anarchy, State and Utopia*, Oxford 1974.

Nuti, M., 'Lessons from Polish Stabilisation', Paper, Trieste 1991.

Nyiri, J.C. and Smith, B., eds, *Practical Knowledge: Outlines of a Theory of Tradition and Skills*, London 1988.

O'Brien, D.J. and Shannon, T.A., eds, *Catholic Social Thought: The Documentary Heritage*, New York 1992.

OECD, *Industry in Poland: Structural Adjustment Issues and Policy Options*, Paris 1992, p. 30.

OECD, *Agricultural Policies, Markets and Trade. Monitoring and Outlook 1994*, Paris 1994.

Offe, C., *Contradictions of the Welfare State*, London 1984.

Ost, D., 'Shock Therapy and its Discontents', *Telos*, No. 92, 1992, pp. 107–12.

Owsiak, S., 'Financial Crisis of the Polish State', in J. Hausner, B. Jessop and K. Nielson, eds. *Strategic Choice and Path-Dependency in Post-Socialism: Institutional Dynamics in the Transformation Process*, Aldershot 1995, pp. 149–67.

Panków, L., *Work Institutions in Transformation: The Case of Poland 1990–92*, Warsaw 1994.

Parnell, M.F., *The German Tradition of Organised Capitalism: Self Government in the Coal Industry*, Oxford 1994.

Patch, W.L., *Christian Trade Unions in the Weimar Republic 1918–1933: The Failure of 'Corporate Pluralism'*, New Haven 1985.

Pelcynski, Z.A., 'The Downfall of Gomulka', in A. Bromke and J.W. Strong, eds, *Gierek's Poland*, New York 1973, pp. 1–23.

Perner, D., *Mitbestimmung im Handwerk? Die politische and soziale Funktion der Handwerkskammern im Geflecht der Unternehmerorganisationen*, Cologne 1983.

Perner, D., 'Die "Reorganisation" der Handwerkskammern in der britischen Besatzungszone nach 1945', in D. Petzina, and W. Euchner, eds, *Wirtschaftspolitik im britischen Besatzungsgebiet 1945–1949*, Düsseldorf 1984.

Pius XI, 'Quadragesimo Anno: Forty Years After *Rerum Novarum*' in O'Brien and Shannon, *Catholic Social Thought*, pp. 42–79.

Polanyi, K., *The Great Transformation: The Political and Economic Origins of Our Time*, Boston 1957.

Polanyi, K., *The Livelihood of Man*, ed. H.W. Pearson, London 1977.

Polanyi, K., 'The Economy as Instituted Process', in *Primitive, Archaic and Modern Economies*, ed. George Dalton, Boston 1968, pp. 139–74.

Polanyi, M., *Personal Knowledge*, London 1958.

Preller, L., *Sozialpolitik in der Weimarer Republik*, Stuttgart 1949.

Prowe, D., 'Economic Democracy in Post-world War II Germany: Corporatist Crisis Response 1945–48', *Journal of Modern History*, Vol. 57, 1985, pp. 451–82.

Rawls, J., *A Theory of Justice*, Oxford 1972.

Rawls, J., 'The Basic Liberties and their Priority', in *The Tanner Lectures on Human Values*, Vol. 3, Cambridge 1982.

Rawls, J., 'Social Unity and Primary Goods', in *Beyond Utilitarianism*, ed. A. Sen. and B. Williams, Cambridge 1982.

Rawls, J., *Political Liberalism*, New York 1993.

Reich, S., *The Fruits of Fascism: Post-war Prosperity in Historical Perspective*, New York 1990, pp. 60–5.

Reynolds, J., 'Communists, Socialists and Workers: Poland 1944–1948', *Soviet Studies*, Vol. 30, No. 4, 1978, pp. 516–39.

Ricardo, D., *On the Principles of Political Economy and Taxation*, eds. P. Sraffa and M.H. Dobb, Cambridge 1951.

Richards, P., 'The State and Early Industrial Capitalism: The Case of the Handloom Weavers', *Past and Present*, No. 83, 1979, pp. 91–115.

Röpke, W., *German Commercial Policy*, London 1934.

Röpke, W., *Die Lehre von der Wirtschaft*, Vienna 1937.

Röpke, W., *International Economic Disintegration*, London 1942.

Röpke, W., *The Social Crisis of Our Time*, (1942), Edinburgh 1950.

Röpke, W., 'Klein- und Mittelbetrieb in der Volkswirtschaft', *ORDO – Jahrbuch für die Ordnung von Wirtschaft und Gesellschaft* Vol. 1, 1948, pp. 155–74.

Röpke, W., *Civitas Humana*, Edinburgh 1949.

Roskamp, K.W., *Capital Formation in West Germany*, Michigan 1965.

Ross, G., Hoffman, S. and Malzacher, S., eds, *The Mitterrand Experiment*, Cambridge 1987.

Rule, J., *The Experience of Labour in Eighteenth Century Industry*, London 1981.

Sabel, C.F., and Stark, D., 'Planning, Politics and Shop-Floor Power: Hidden Forms of Bargaining in Soviet-Imposed State-Socialist Societies', *Politics and Society*, Vol. 11, No. 4, 1982, pp. 439–75.

Sabel, C.F. and Zeitlin, J., 'Historical Alternatives to Mass Production: Politics, Markets and Technology in Nineteenth Century Industrialisation', *Past and Present*, No. 108, 1985, pp. 133–76.

Sachs, J. and Wyplosz, C., 'The Economic Consequences of Mitterrand's Economic Policy', in M. Bruno and J. Sachs, eds, *Economics of Worldwide Stagflation*, Cambridge Mass. 1986.

Sachs, J., *Poland's Jump to the Market Economy*, London 1994.

Sachs, J., *Understanding Shock Therapy*, London 1994.

Sandowski, D., 'The Finance and Governance of the German Apprenticeship System', *Journal of Institutional and Theoretical Economics*, Vol. 137, No. 2, pp. 234–51.

Saville, J., *1848: The British State and the Chartist Movement*, Cambridge 1987.

Schanze, E., and Haunhorst, K.H., 'Security of Tenure in Conventional and "Flexible" Employment regimes – A Neo-Institutional Perspective', paper presented at the conference 'Labour Market Institutions and Constraints', EUI Florence, May 1993.

Schneider, M., *Die Christlichen Gewerkschaften 1894–1933*, Bonn 1982.

Schurmann, F., *The Logic of World Power: An Inquiry into the Origins, Currents and Contradictions of World Politics*, New York 1974.

Scruton, R., *The Meaning of Conservatism*, London 1984.

Sewell, W.H. Jr., *Work and Revolution in France: The Language of Labour from the Old Regime to 1848*, Cambridge 1981.

Shapiro, I., 'The Fiscal Crisis of the Polish State: Genesis of the 1980 Strikes', *Theory and Society*, Vol. 10, No. 4, 1981, pp. 469–502.

Sigmund, P.E., 'The Catholic Tradition and Modern Democracy', *Review of Politics*, Vol. 49, No. 4, 1987, pp. 530–48.

Singer, D., *The Road To Gdansk*, London 1982.

Singer, D., *Is Socialism Doomed?*, Oxford 1991.

Smith, E.O., *The German Economy*, London 1994.

Smith, S.C., 'On the Economic Rationale of Co-determination Law', *Journal of Economic Behaviour and Organisation*, Vol. 16, 1991, pp. 261–81.

Solidarity, 'Programme adopted by the First National Congress' in Peter Raina, ed., *Poland 1981: Towards Social Renewal*, London 1981, pp. 326–90.

Sorge, A. and Streeck, W., 'Industrial Relations and Technical Change: The Case for an Extended Perspective', in R. Hyman and W. Streeck, eds, *New Technology and Industrial Relations*, Oxford 1988, pp. 19–47.

Soskice, D., 'Reconciling Markets and Institutions: The German Apprenticeship System', in L. Lynch, ed., *Training and the Private Sector: International Comparisons*, Chicago 1993.

Spence, T., 'The Real Rights of Man', in *The Political Work of Thomas Spence*, ed. H.T. Dickinson, Newcastle Upon Tyne 1982.

Stadelmann, R., *Social and Political History of the German 1848 Revolution*, Ohio 1975.

Steinmetz, G., *Regulating the Social: The Welfare State and Local Politics in Imperial Germany*, Princeton 1993.

Streeck, W., *The Role of the Social Partners in Vocational Training and Further Training*, Berlin 1987.

Streeck, W., *Social Institutions and Economic Performance: Studies of Industrial Relations in Advanced Capitalist Economies*, London 1992.

Streeck, W., 'Productive Constraints: On the Institutional Conditions of Diversified Quality Production', in *Social Institutions and Economic Performance*, pp. 1–40.

Streeck, W., 'The Logics of Associative Action and the Territorial Organisation of Interests: The Case of German Handwerk', in *Social Institutions and Economic Performance*, pp. 105–36.

Streeck, W., 'Co-determination after Four Decades', in *Social Institutions and Economic Performance*, pp. 137–69.

Streeck, W., 'Beneficial Constraints: On the Economic Limits of Rational Voluntarism', Conference Paper, New York 1993.

Surdej, A., 'Politics and the Stabilisation Plan', Cracow Academy of Economics Seminar Paper No. 9, 1992.

Szporluk, R., *Communism and Nationalism: Karl Marx Versus Friedrich List*, Oxford 1988.

Tampke, J., *The Ruhr and Revolution: The Revolutionary Movement in the Rhenish Westphalia Industrial Region 1912–1919*, London 1979.

Tampke, J., 'Bismarck's Social Legislation: A Genuine Breakthrough?', in W.J. Mommsen, ed., *The Emergence of the Welfare State in Britain and Germany, 1850–1950*, London 1981, pp. 71–83.

Taras, R., *Ideology in a Socialist State: Poland 1956–1983*, Cambridge 1984.

Thompson, E.P., *The Making of the English Working Class*, New York 1963.

Thompson, E.P., 'The Moral Economy of the English Crowd in the Eighteenth Century', *Past and Present*, No. 50, 1971, pp. 76–136.

Thompson, N., *The People's Science: The Popular Political Economy of Exploitation and Crisis 1816–1834*, Cambridge 1984.

Tittenbrun, J., *The Collapse of Real Socialism in Poland*, London 1993.

Tomann, H., 'The Housing Market, Housing Finance and Housing Policy in West Germany', *Urban Studies*, Vol. 27, No. 6, 1990, pp. 919–30.

Townsend, J., *Dissertation on the Poor Laws*, London 1776.

Tribe, K., *Strategies of Economic Order: German Economic Discourse 1750–1950*. Cambridge 1995.

Tribe, K., 'The Genealogy of the Social Market Economy: 1937–48', in *Strategies of Economic Order*, pp. 203–40.

Tribe, K., 'The New Economic Order and European Economic Integration' in *Strategies of Economic Order*, pp. 241–62.

Tuchtfeld, E., 'Handwerk', in *Staatslexikon: Rechtswissenschaft – Gesellschaft*, Freiburg 1986.

Tudor, H. and Tudor, J.M., *Marxism and Social-Democracy: The Revisionist Debate*, Cambridge 1988.

Turner, S., *The Social Theory of Practices: Tradition, Tacit Knowledge and Presuppositions*, Chicago 1994.

Uhl, B., *Die Idee des Christlichen Sozialismus in Deutschland, 1945–1947*, Mainz 1975.

UNICEF, *Economies in Transition Studies, Regional Monitoring Report, 1994. Crisis in Mortality, Health and Nutrition*, Florence 1994.

Untersted, R., *Mittelstand in der Weimarer Republik: Die Soziale Entwicklung und Politische Orientierung von Handwerk, Kleinhandel und Hausbesitz, 1919–1937*, Frankfurt 1989.

Useem, M., *The Inner Circle: Large Corporations and the Rise of Business Political Activity in the US and UK*, Oxford 1984.

Van Kersbergen, K., 'The Distinctiveness of Christian Democracy', in David Hanley, ed., *Christian Democracy in Europe: A Comparative Perspective*, London 1994, pp. 31–50.

Van Kersbergen, K., *Social Capitalism: A Study of Christian Democracy and the Welfare State*, London 1996.

Van Parijs, P., ed., *Arguing for Basic Income*, London 1992.

Volkov, S., *The Rise of Popular Anti-modernism in Germany: The Urban Master Artisans 1873–1896*, Princeton 1978.

Von Oertzen, P., *Betriebsräte in der Novemberrevolution*, Düsseldorf 1963.

Von Saldern, A., 'The Old *Mittelstand* 1890–1933: How "Backward" Were the Artisans?', *Central European History*, Vol. 25, No. 1, 1992, pp. 27–51.

Walker, M., *German Home Towns: Community, State and General Estate 1648–1871*, Ithaca 1971.

Walther, R., 'Economic Liberalism', *Economy and Society*, Vol. 13, No. 2, 1984, pp. 178–207.

Waterman, A.M.C., 'John Locke's Theory of Property and Christian Social Thought', *Review of Social Economy*, Vol. 40, 1982, pp. 97–115.

Wedel, J.R., 'The Unintended Consequences of Western Aid to Post-Communist Europe', *Telos*, No. 92, 1992, pp. 131–8.

Wernet, W., *Handwerkspolitik*, Göttingen 1972.

Williams, L., 'Ideological Parallels between the New Left and New Right', *Social Science Journal*, Vol. 24, 1987, pp. 317–27.

Wilson, E., *A Very British Miracle*, London 1992.

Winkler, H.A., 'From Social Protection to National Socialism: The German Small Business Movement in Comparative Perspective', *Journal of Modern History*, Vol. 48, 1976.

Winkler, H.A., 'Stabilisierung durch Schrumpfung: Der gewerbliche Mittelstand in der Bundesrepublik', in W. Conze and M.R. Lepsius, eds, *Sozialgeschichte der Bundesrepublik Deutschland*, Stuttgart 1983.

Wolf, H.C., 'The Lucky Miracle: Germany 1945–1951', in R. Dornbusch, W. Nölling and R. Layard, eds, *Post-war Reconstruction and Lessons for the East Today*, Cambridge Mass. 1993, pp. 29–56.

Wolin, S.S., *Politics and Vision*, New York 1960.

Wordie, J.R., 'The Chronology of English Enclosure, 1500–1914', *Economic History Review*, Second Series, 1983.

World Bank Report on Poverty in Poland: Vol. 1, Washington 1994.

Yenger, C.B., *International Monetary Relations*, New York 1976.

Yonke, E., 'The Catholic Sub-Culture in Modern Germany: Recent Work in the Social History of Religion', *Catholic Historical Review*, Vol. 80, No. 3, 1994.

Young, M., 'Malthus and the Evolutionists: The Common Context of Biological and Social Theory', *Past and Present*, No. 43, 1969.

Zeitlin, J., 'From Labour History to the History of Industrial Relations', *Economic History Review*, Vol. 40, No. 2, 1987, pp. 159–84.

Zoeter, J., 'Eastern Europe: The Hard Currency Debt', *East European Economic Assessment*, Washington DC 1981.

Index

Also of interest
from Verso

Mapping the West European Left
Edited by Perry Anderson and Patrick Camiller

A Zone of Engagement
Perry Anderson

The Long Twentieth Century
Money, Power, and the Origins of Our Times
Giovanni Arrighi

Associations and Democracy
The Real Utopias Project Volume I
Edited and Introduced by Joshua Cohen and Joel Rogers

Solidarity in the Conversation of Humankind
The Ungroundable Liberalism of Richard Rorty
Norman Geras

Capitalism, Socialism, Ecology
André Gorz
Translated by Chris Turner

Critique of Economic Reason
André Gorz
Translated by Gillian Handyside and Chris Turner

Autonomy and Solidarity
Interviews with Jürgen Habermas
Edited and Introduced by Peter Dews

Reflections on Violence
John Keane

Critique of Everyday Life
Henri Lefebvre
Translated by John Moore

Introduction to Modernity
Henri Lefebvre
Translated by John Moore

Posthistoire
Has History Come to an End?
Lutz Niethammer
Translated by Patrick Camiller

A Future for Socialism
John E. Roemer

Equal Shares
Making Market Socialism Work
The Real Utopias Project Volume II
John E. Roemer
Edited and Introduced by Erik Olin Wright

Karl Kautsky and the Socialist Revolution 1880–1938
Massimo Salvadori
Translated by Jon Rothschild